# Digital Detectives: Strategies for Uncovering Cybercrime Evidence

Dmitry Popovyzu

**Dmitry Popovyzu** is a seasoned cybersecurity expert and digital forensics specialist with over a decade of experience in the field. With a background in computer science and a passion for technology, Dmitry has dedicated his career to understanding the complexities of cybercrime and the evolving landscape of digital threats.

Having worked with law enforcement agencies, private corporations, and non-profit organizations, he has gained a unique perspective on the intricacies of cyber investigations and the vital role they play in safeguarding society. His hands-on experience includes conducting digital forensic analyses, developing incident response strategies, and providing training on the latest cybersecurity practices.

Dmitry's commitment to knowledge-sharing extends beyond his professional engagements; he frequently writes articles and speaks at conferences about the importance of digital literacy, cybersecurity awareness, and effective investigation techniques. His deep understanding of both the technical and legal aspects of cybercrime makes him a trusted voice in the industry.

In **Digital Detectives: Strategies for Uncovering Cybercrime Evidence**, Dmitry aims to equip readers—whether they are aspiring investigators, seasoned professionals, or simply curious individuals—with the tools and strategies needed to navigate the complex world of cybercrime. Drawing from real-world case studies and the latest research, he provides actionable insights that can empower anyone to become a more effective digital detective.

Join Dmitry on this journey as he explores the multifaceted nature of cybercrime and offers practical guidance for uncovering the evidence that can lead to justice in the digital age.

In an age where digital interactions dominate our daily lives, the threat of cybercrime has never been more pressing. From data breaches and identity theft to cyberbullying and ransomware attacks, the digital landscape poses significant risks to individuals and organizations alike. As technology continues to evolve, so too do the tactics employed by cybercriminals, making it essential for those on the front lines—law enforcement, cybersecurity professionals, and even everyday citizens—to stay informed and equipped to combat these threats.

**Digital Detectives: Strategies for Uncovering Cybercrime Evidence** serves as a comprehensive guide to navigating the intricate world of cybercrime investigations. This book combines theoretical insights with practical strategies, offering readers the tools needed to uncover digital evidence and effectively respond to cyber incidents.

Through a blend of real-world case studies, expert interviews, and actionable techniques, this book aims to empower a new generation of digital detectives. Whether you are a seasoned professional looking to enhance your skills or a novice seeking to understand the basics, this book provides valuable insights into the art and science of cybercrime investigation.

## Chapter 1: The Evolution of Cybercrime

This chapter provides a historical overview of cybercrime, tracing its roots from early computer hacking to the sophisticated organized cybercriminal networks of today. Understanding this evolution is crucial for recognizing the ongoing challenges and threats in the digital landscape.

## Chapter 2: Understanding Cybercrime Frameworks

In this chapter, we explore key frameworks that guide cybercrime investigations. From the Cyber Kill Chain to the MITRE ATT&CK framework, these models provide a structured approach for analyzing and responding to cyber threats.

## Chapter 3: Digital Forensics Fundamentals

This chapter introduces the foundational concepts of digital forensics, including the types of digital evidence and the forensic process. Readers will gain a clear understanding of what digital forensics entails and its critical role in cyber investigations.

## Chapter 4: Collecting Evidence: Tools and Techniques

In this chapter, we delve into the practical aspects of evidence collection, including various tools and techniques. Emphasis is placed on maintaining the integrity of evidence and following proper protocols to ensure admissibility in court.

**Chapter 5: Analyzing Digital Evidence**

This chapter focuses on the analysis of digital evidence, covering methods such as file system analysis, network traffic monitoring, and malware investigation. Readers will learn how to identify key indicators of cybercrime through systematic analysis.

**Chapter 6: Legal Considerations in Cyber Investigations**

Understanding the legal landscape is essential for any cyber investigator. This chapter discusses relevant laws, ethical considerations, and the importance of data privacy in the context of cybercrime investigations.

**Chapter 7: Case Studies in Cybercrime Investigations**

This chapter features real-world case studies that highlight successful cybercrime investigations. By analyzing these cases, readers will gain insight into effective strategies and the challenges investigators face in the field.

**Chapter 8: Social Media and Cybercrime**

Social media platforms are both a tool for criminals and a source of evidence for investigators. This chapter explores the relationship between social media and cybercrime, highlighting methods for gathering and analyzing evidence from these platforms.

**Chapter 9: Incident Response Planning**

Effective incident response is key to minimizing damage from cyber incidents. This chapter outlines the steps to create an incident response plan, including team roles, response procedures, and post-incident evaluations.

**Chapter 10: Emerging Technologies and Cyber Threats**

As technology advances, so do the threats that accompany it. This chapter examines emerging technologies—such as AI, IoT, and blockchain—and their implications for cybersecurity and investigation strategies.

**Chapter 11: Building a Cybercrime Investigation Team**

The success of cybercrime investigations often hinges on the team behind them. This chapter discusses the skills and training necessary for assembling a competent investigation team and the importance of collaboration with various stakeholders.

**Chapter 12: Future Trends in Cybercrime and Investigation**

In the concluding chapter, we look ahead to the future of cybercrime, exploring potential threats and the evolving strategies that investigators will need to adopt. This forward-thinking approach prepares readers to anticipate and respond to new challenges in the digital landscape.

# Chapter 1: The Evolution of Cybercrime

In this chapter, we embark on a journey through the history of cybercrime, exploring its origins and transformation over the decades. From the early days of simple hacks and pranks in the 1970s and 1980s to the emergence of sophisticated criminal organizations in the digital age, we will trace the key developments that have shaped the landscape of cyber threats today. By understanding how cybercrime has evolved, readers will gain valuable insights into the motivations and tactics of cybercriminals, laying the groundwork for effective strategies to combat these threats in the modern world.

## 1.1 Early Cyber Crimes: A Historical Perspective

The concept of cybercrime may seem like a product of the digital age, but its roots trace back to the early days of computing and networking. As technology evolved, so too did the methods of exploitation and criminal behavior. Understanding early cyber crimes provides valuable context for today's threats and illustrates how cybercriminals have adapted to technological advancements. This exploration encompasses the origins of computer hacking, significant incidents that shaped the field, and the legal and societal responses to these early forms of cybercrime.

**The Dawn of Computing**

The late 20th century marked the advent of personal computing, beginning in the 1970s with the introduction of microcomputers. As computers became more accessible, individuals began to experiment with programming and networking. The burgeoning interest in computer technology fostered a sense of community among early adopters, often characterized by a spirit of exploration and curiosity. However, this environment also laid the groundwork for the emergence of cybercriminal behavior.

Early hacking was often driven by curiosity, with individuals seeking to understand how systems operated rather than with malicious intent. One of the earliest known instances of hacking occurred in 1983 when a group of students gained unauthorized access to the ARPANET, a precursor to the internet. This event marked a significant moment in the history of cybercrime, demonstrating that even the most secure networks were vulnerable to exploitation.

**The 1980s: The Birth of Hacking Culture**

The 1980s saw the rise of a distinct hacking culture, characterized by the sharing of knowledge and techniques among enthusiasts. One of the most influential works of this era was "The Hacker's Handbook," published in 1986 by the hacker group Legion of Doom. This publication, along with others, helped to popularize hacking and introduced techniques for exploiting vulnerabilities in computer systems.

Around this time, the term "hacker" began to take on a dual meaning. While some hackers were motivated by curiosity and the pursuit of knowledge, others used their skills for malicious purposes. This period also saw the rise of "phone phreaking," where individuals manipulated telephone systems to make free calls. This practice was an early form of cybercrime that highlighted the vulnerabilities in communication networks and set a precedent for future cybercriminal activities.

**Significant Incidents and Legal Responses**

As hacking became more prevalent, it drew the attention of law enforcement and lawmakers. In 1986, the U.S. Congress passed the Computer Fraud and Abuse Act (CFAA), a landmark piece of legislation aimed at addressing unauthorized access to computer systems. The CFAA represented a significant step toward recognizing cybercrime as a serious offense, establishing penalties for various forms of computer-related crimes.

One of the most notorious incidents of this era was the 1989 "Mafiaboy" attack. A 15-year-old hacker known as Mafiaboy infiltrated several high-profile websites, including those of CNN, Dell, and eBay, causing significant disruptions. This incident not only highlighted the vulnerabilities of major corporations but also underscored the need for stronger cybersecurity measures. Mafiaboy's arrest and subsequent legal consequences further solidified the notion that cybercrime would be treated seriously in the eyes of the law.

**The 1990s: The Emergence of Malware**

The 1990s ushered in a new era of cybercrime with the rise of malware, which refers to malicious software designed to disrupt, damage, or gain unauthorized access to computer systems. One of the most infamous examples of early malware was the "ILOVEYOU" virus, which spread rapidly in 2000 through email attachments. This worm infected millions of computers worldwide, causing billions of dollars in damages. The ILOVEYOU virus was a wake-up call for individuals and organizations alike, demonstrating the destructive potential of malware and the necessity for effective cybersecurity practices.

During this period, the internet began to grow exponentially, leading to an increase in online interactions and transactions. This growth created new opportunities for cybercriminals to exploit vulnerabilities in online systems, paving the way for various forms of cybercrime, including identity theft and online fraud. The expansion of the internet also prompted the development of cybersecurity technologies and practices, as individuals and businesses sought to protect themselves from emerging threats.

**The Role of the Media and Public Perception**

As incidents of cybercrime garnered media attention, public perception began to shift. High-profile hacks and data breaches were often sensationalized, contributing to a growing fear of cyber threats. This fear was not entirely unfounded, as cybercriminals became more sophisticated in their methods. The media's portrayal of hackers, often as antiheroes or vigilantes, further complicated the narrative surrounding cybercrime.

The portrayal of hackers in films and television also played a role in shaping public perception. Movies like "WarGames" (1983) and "Hackers" (1995) romanticized hacking culture while raising awareness of the potential risks associated with technology. These representations contributed to a broader conversation about the ethical implications of hacking and the need for a balanced understanding of the hacker ethos.

**The Turn of the Millennium: Cybercrime Becomes Organized**

As we entered the 21st century, cybercrime began to take on a more organized and commercialized form. Criminal groups started to collaborate, sharing tools and techniques to execute more sophisticated attacks. The emergence of the dark web provided a new platform for illicit activities, allowing cybercriminals to trade stolen data, hacking services, and malware.

One significant event in this era was the 2007 cyberattack on Estonia, which targeted the country's government, banks, and media outlets. This attack demonstrated the potential for cyber warfare and highlighted the importance of cybersecurity on a national level. The Estonian attack also led to increased international collaboration in addressing cyber threats, as nations recognized the need for collective action to combat cybercrime.

The historical perspective of early cyber crimes reveals a dynamic evolution of criminal behavior alongside technological advancements. From the curiosity-driven explorations of early hackers to the organized and sophisticated cybercrime of today, the landscape has changed dramatically. Understanding this history not only sheds light on the origins of current cyber threats but also underscores the necessity for continued vigilance and innovation in cybersecurity practices.

As we progress further into the digital age, it is essential to recognize that cybercrime is a constantly evolving phenomenon. By learning from the past, we can better prepare for the future, equipping ourselves with the knowledge and tools necessary to combat the ever-changing landscape of cyber threats. The journey from early cybercrime to the complex threats we face today serves as a reminder of the ongoing battle between technological innovation and the dark forces seeking to exploit it.

## 1.2 The Rise of Organized Cybercrime

The evolution of cybercrime has progressed from individual hackers motivated by curiosity or mischief to sophisticated networks of organized crime that exploit digital technologies for financial gain. This transformation represents a significant shift in the landscape of cybercrime, reflecting both the growing accessibility of technology and the increasing complexity of criminal operations. Understanding the rise of organized cybercrime is essential for developing effective countermeasures and recognizing the societal impacts of these illicit activities.

**The Transition from Individual to Organized Crime**

In the early days of hacking, many offenders operated independently, motivated by personal curiosity or the thrill of breaking into secure systems. However, as technology advanced and the internet became a global network, the potential for profit from cybercrime attracted more organized groups. Criminal enterprises began to recognize that cybercrime offered lower risks compared to traditional crime, such as drug trafficking or robbery, while providing significant financial rewards.

This shift marked the birth of organized cybercrime, characterized by well-defined roles within criminal organizations, including hackers, fraudsters, and money launderers. These groups often collaborate across borders, leveraging the anonymity of the internet to operate outside the reach of law enforcement. By sharing tools, techniques, and resources, organized cybercriminals can execute large-scale operations that target individuals, businesses, and governments alike.

**Key Characteristics of Organized Cybercrime**

Organized cybercrime shares several key characteristics that distinguish it from individual hacking:

**Structure and Hierarchy**: Organized cybercriminal groups often resemble traditional criminal organizations, with a clear hierarchy and division of labor. This structure allows for more efficient operations and the ability to carry out complex schemes that require specialized skills.

**Financial Motivation**: Unlike early hackers, who often engaged in cyber activities for personal satisfaction or notoriety, organized cybercriminals are primarily motivated by profit. They utilize various methods to monetize their activities, including ransomware attacks, credit card fraud, and identity theft.

**Global Reach**: The internet enables organized cybercrime to transcend geographical boundaries, allowing criminal groups to operate internationally. This global nature complicates law enforcement efforts, as different jurisdictions may have varying laws and enforcement capabilities.

**Use of Advanced Technology**: Organized cybercriminals leverage sophisticated technology and techniques, including encryption, anonymization tools, and malware, to evade detection and increase the effectiveness of their operations. They also invest in research and development to stay ahead of cybersecurity measures.

**The Role of the Dark Web**

The dark web has played a pivotal role in the rise of organized cybercrime by providing a platform for illicit activities to flourish. This hidden part of the internet is accessible only through specialized browsers, allowing users to remain anonymous and conduct illegal transactions with relative safety. Criminals have established forums and marketplaces on the dark web where they can buy and sell stolen data, hacking tools, and services such as distributed denial-of-service (DDoS) attacks.

For instance, platforms like Silk Road revolutionized online drug trafficking, while similar sites have emerged for a wide range of illicit goods and services, including hacking services, counterfeit currency, and stolen credentials. The anonymity and ease of use of dark web marketplaces have facilitated the growth of organized cybercrime, enabling groups to connect, collaborate, and carry out their operations more efficiently.

**Notable Examples of Organized Cybercrime**

Several high-profile cases exemplify the rise of organized cybercrime and its impact on society:

**Russian Cybercrime Groups**: Groups like REvil and Fancy Bear have gained notoriety for their sophisticated ransomware attacks and state-sponsored hacking activities. REvil, for example, has been responsible for high-profile ransomware attacks against organizations like Kaseya and JBS, demanding millions in ransom. Their ability to operate from countries with lax cybersecurity laws demonstrates the challenges faced by international law enforcement.

**The Carbanak Gang**: This criminal organization targeted banks and financial institutions worldwide, stealing over $1 billion from victims through a series of carefully orchestrated attacks. By infiltrating banking networks and manipulating internal systems, the Carbanak gang exemplified the advanced techniques employed by organized cybercriminals.

**Business Email Compromise (BEC)**: BEC scams have become a common tactic employed by organized crime groups, targeting companies by impersonating executives or trusted partners to trick employees into transferring funds. These scams often involve extensive research and planning, showcasing the organizational skills of these criminal enterprises.

**Societal Impacts and Consequences**

The rise of organized cybercrime has far-reaching consequences for individuals, businesses, and society as a whole. As these criminal networks become more sophisticated, the impact of their activities becomes increasingly severe:

**Financial Losses**: Organizations face significant financial losses due to cybercrime, with estimates running into billions of dollars each year. These losses not only affect the targeted companies but also have broader economic implications, including job losses and reduced consumer confidence.

**Data Breaches**: Organized cybercriminals often target sensitive data, leading to large-scale breaches that compromise personal information, including credit card details and social security numbers. Such breaches can have lasting effects on victims, including identity theft and financial ruin.

**Disruption of Services**: Ransomware attacks targeting critical infrastructure, such as healthcare, energy, and transportation, can lead to widespread disruption and threaten public safety. For example, the Colonial Pipeline attack in 2021 resulted in fuel shortages and raised concerns about the vulnerability of essential services to cyber threats.

**Erosion of Trust**: As cybercrime becomes more prevalent, public trust in online systems and services may decline. Individuals may hesitate to engage in online transactions or share personal information, stunting the growth of e-commerce and digital services.

**Law Enforcement Responses**

In response to the rise of organized cybercrime, law enforcement agencies worldwide have increased their efforts to combat these threats. Collaborative initiatives, such as the FBI's Cyber Task Forces and the European Union Agency for Cybersecurity (ENISA), aim to share intelligence, coordinate investigations, and develop effective strategies to disrupt criminal networks.

International cooperation is vital in addressing organized cybercrime, as many groups operate across borders. Agencies are working together to strengthen legal frameworks, enhance information sharing, and conduct joint operations to dismantle cybercriminal organizations.

The rise of organized cybercrime represents a significant evolution in the landscape of cyber threats, characterized by structured networks that exploit digital technologies for profit. As technology continues to advance, so too will the methods employed by these criminal enterprises. Understanding the dynamics of organized cybercrime is essential for developing effective countermeasures and fostering collaboration among law enforcement, cybersecurity professionals, and the private sector.

As society becomes increasingly reliant on digital technologies, the challenge of combating organized cybercrime will remain a pressing concern. By recognizing the threat posed by these criminal networks and investing in proactive measures, we can better protect individuals, businesses, and critical infrastructure from the pervasive risks associated with organized cybercrime.

## 1.3 Emerging Threats in the Digital Age

The rapid evolution of technology has given rise to a new generation of cyber threats that are increasingly sophisticated, diverse, and impactful. As digital systems become more integrated into daily life, from personal devices to critical infrastructure, the potential attack surface for cybercriminals expands dramatically. This chapter explores the emerging threats in the digital age, highlighting the motivations behind these threats, the technologies facilitating them, and the potential consequences for individuals and organizations alike.

## 1. The Evolution of Cyber Threats

Historically, cyber threats were often motivated by curiosity, political activism, or a desire for notoriety. However, as the financial stakes of cybercrime have increased, so too have the motivations behind these attacks. Today, cybercriminals are primarily driven by financial gain, political objectives, or even ideological beliefs. This shift in motivation has led to the development of more organized and complex cybercriminal operations, often backed by sophisticated technologies and methodologies.

## 2. Key Emerging Threats

As we navigate the digital landscape, several key threats have emerged, reshaping the cybersecurity environment:

### A. Ransomware Attacks

Ransomware has emerged as one of the most pressing threats in the digital age. In these attacks, cybercriminals infiltrate a victim's system, encrypt their data, and demand a ransom for the decryption key. High-profile incidents, such as the Colonial Pipeline attack in 2021 and the JBS Foods attack, have underscored the devastating impact of ransomware on critical infrastructure and the economy. These attacks often exploit vulnerabilities in software or human error, making prevention and response increasingly challenging.

### B. Phishing and Social Engineering

Phishing attacks continue to evolve in sophistication, often utilizing social engineering tactics to manipulate individuals into divulging sensitive information. Cybercriminals craft convincing emails or messages that impersonate trusted sources, making it difficult for victims to recognize the threat. As remote work becomes more prevalent, attackers have tailored their strategies to exploit this shift, targeting employees working outside secure corporate environments.

### C. Internet of Things (IoT) Vulnerabilities

The proliferation of IoT devices has opened new avenues for cyber threats. Many IoT devices lack robust security features, making them susceptible to exploitation. Cybercriminals can leverage compromised IoT devices to launch attacks, infiltrate networks, or create botnets for Distributed Denial-of-Service (DDoS) attacks. The interconnected nature of IoT devices means that a single vulnerability can have cascading effects, potentially compromising entire systems.

**D. Artificial Intelligence (AI) and Machine Learning Threats**

While AI and machine learning offer tremendous potential for improving cybersecurity, they can also be weaponized by cybercriminals. Attackers can use AI algorithms to automate attacks, analyze vast amounts of data to identify vulnerabilities, and create highly convincing phishing campaigns. Additionally, adversarial AI techniques can be employed to bypass traditional security measures, making detection and prevention increasingly difficult.

**E. Deepfakes and Misinformation**

The rise of deepfake technology poses significant risks, particularly in terms of misinformation and social manipulation. Deepfakes, which use AI to create realistic but fabricated audio and video content, can be employed to spread false narratives, manipulate public opinion, or even blackmail individuals. The potential for deepfakes to erode trust in media and institutions presents a unique challenge for society, as distinguishing between reality and deception becomes increasingly difficult.

**3. The Impact of Emerging Threats**

The consequences of emerging cyber threats can be severe, affecting individuals, organizations, and society as a whole:

**Financial Loss**: The financial impact of cybercrime is staggering, with global losses estimated in the trillions annually. Ransomware attacks, in particular, have resulted in significant financial damages for victims, not to mention the costs associated with recovery and legal repercussions.

**Data Breaches**: Emerging threats often lead to data breaches, compromising sensitive information such as personal identification, financial data, and intellectual property. The fallout from data breaches can include reputational damage, regulatory fines, and legal liabilities.

**Erosion of Trust**: As cyber threats become more prevalent and sophisticated, public trust in digital systems may wane. Individuals and organizations may hesitate to adopt new technologies or engage in online transactions, stifling innovation and economic growth.

**Disruption of Services**: Cyberattacks targeting critical infrastructure, such as healthcare, transportation, and energy, can lead to widespread disruption and public safety concerns. For instance, a ransomware attack on a hospital can hinder patient care, endangering lives and eroding public confidence in essential services.

### 4. Strategies for Mitigation

Addressing emerging cyber threats requires a proactive and multi-faceted approach:

#### A. Strengthening Cyber Hygiene

Promoting good cyber hygiene practices among individuals and organizations is essential. This includes regular software updates, using strong and unique passwords, and educating users about recognizing phishing attempts and social engineering tactics.

#### B. Investing in Advanced Security Solutions

Organizations should invest in advanced cybersecurity technologies, such as AI-driven threat detection systems, endpoint protection, and incident response solutions. These technologies can help identify and mitigate threats before they cause significant damage.

#### C. Collaboration and Information Sharing

Collaboration among industry stakeholders, government agencies, and law enforcement is crucial for combating emerging threats. Information sharing initiatives can help organizations stay informed about new threats and vulnerabilities, enabling them to respond effectively.

#### D. Developing Incident Response Plans

Establishing comprehensive incident response plans is vital for organizations to quickly address and mitigate the impact of cyber incidents. These plans should include clear protocols for communication, recovery, and post-incident analysis to improve future defenses.

Emerging threats in the digital age pose significant challenges for individuals, organizations, and society as a whole. As cybercriminals become increasingly sophisticated and organized, the need for effective cybersecurity measures has never been more critical. Understanding the landscape of emerging threats is essential for developing proactive strategies that can mitigate risks and safeguard our digital lives.

By fostering a culture of cybersecurity awareness, investing in advanced technologies, and promoting collaboration among stakeholders, we can work together to combat the evolving threat landscape and build a safer digital future. As technology continues to advance, the battle against cybercrime will require ongoing vigilance, innovation, and adaptation to stay one step ahead of those who seek to exploit it.

# Chapter 2: Understanding Cybercrime Frameworks

In this chapter, we delve into the essential frameworks that provide structure and guidance for cybercrime investigations. These frameworks, including the Cyber Kill Chain and the MITRE ATT&CK framework, offer investigators a systematic approach to understanding the stages of cyber attacks and the tactics used by adversaries. By breaking down complex cyber incidents into manageable components, these models help identify vulnerabilities, anticipate potential threats, and develop effective countermeasures. As we explore each framework, we will highlight their practical applications in real-world investigations, empowering readers to utilize these tools to enhance their own cyber defense strategies and investigative capabilities.

## 2.1 The Cyber Kill Chain: Understanding the Attack Lifecycle

The Cyber Kill Chain is a conceptual framework that outlines the stages of a cyberattack, enabling organizations to better understand, detect, and respond to potential threats. Developed by Lockheed Martin, the model categorizes the phases of an attack into distinct steps, providing a structured approach to cybersecurity that can help organizations bolster their defenses and improve their incident response strategies. By understanding the cyber kill chain, security professionals can identify vulnerabilities, implement preventive measures, and respond more effectively to incidents.

**Overview of the Cyber Kill Chain**

The Cyber Kill Chain consists of seven stages that represent the lifecycle of a cyberattack, from initial reconnaissance to the final objectives. Each stage is critical in understanding how attackers operate and where organizations can intervene to thwart their efforts.

**Reconnaissance**: This initial phase involves gathering information about the target. Attackers conduct reconnaissance to identify potential vulnerabilities, discover valuable assets, and understand the target's network architecture. Techniques used in this phase may include social engineering, open-source intelligence (OSINT), and scanning for vulnerabilities in publicly accessible systems. Organizations can mitigate risks during this phase by implementing strict access controls, monitoring external communications, and regularly reviewing their public-facing assets for exposure.

**Weaponization**: In this stage, attackers create a malicious payload that will be delivered to the target. This can involve developing malware, such as viruses, worms, or ransomware, often packaged with a delivery mechanism like a phishing email or exploit kit. For instance, attackers may create a document with embedded macros that download malware once opened. Understanding the methods attackers use to weaponize their attacks allows organizations to develop robust email filtering and anti-malware solutions to detect and block these threats before they reach their intended targets.

**Delivery**: The delivery phase refers to the transmission of the weaponized payload to the target. This can occur through various channels, including phishing emails, malicious attachments, or compromised websites. The effectiveness of this stage often relies on the success of the previous reconnaissance and weaponization steps. Organizations can improve their defenses during this phase by implementing email filtering, employee training programs on recognizing phishing attempts, and establishing web filtering mechanisms to block access to known malicious sites.

**Exploitation**: Once the payload has been delivered, attackers exploit vulnerabilities within the target's system to execute the malicious code. This could involve leveraging known software vulnerabilities, exploiting weak passwords, or using social engineering techniques to trick users into granting access. Security measures like patch management, regular system updates, and user awareness training can help mitigate exploitation risks by closing known vulnerabilities and reducing the likelihood of successful attacks.

**Installation**: Following successful exploitation, attackers aim to install malware on the target system to establish a foothold within the network. This could involve installing remote access tools (RATs) or backdoors that allow the attacker to maintain persistent access even if the initial exploit is detected and remediated. Organizations can combat this by employing endpoint detection and response (EDR) solutions, which monitor for unusual behavior and unauthorized software installations.

**Command and Control (C2):** In this stage, the attacker establishes a communication channel with the compromised system, allowing them to remotely control it and issue commands. Command and control infrastructures can be designed to evade detection, often using encrypted communication or dynamic domain generation. Organizations can enhance their defenses against C2 attempts by monitoring network traffic for unusual patterns, implementing intrusion detection systems (IDS), and blocking known malicious IP addresses.

**Actions on Objectives**: The final phase of the Cyber Kill Chain involves the attacker executing their primary goals, which can include data exfiltration, financial theft, sabotage, or other malicious actions. Once the attacker achieves their objectives, they may attempt to cover their tracks to avoid detection. Understanding the potential objectives of cybercriminals allows organizations to prioritize their security efforts and develop tailored response plans for various attack scenarios.

**The Importance of the Cyber Kill Chain**

Understanding the Cyber Kill Chain provides organizations with several key benefits:

**Enhanced Threat Detection**: By identifying the specific stages of an attack, organizations can implement targeted detection measures at each phase, improving their chances of catching an attack before it reaches its final objective.

**Proactive Defense Strategies**: The Cyber Kill Chain encourages a proactive approach to cybersecurity, prompting organizations to think like attackers and anticipate potential threats. This mindset can help inform security policies, incident response plans, and employee training programs.

**Improved Incident Response**: With a clear understanding of the attack lifecycle, security teams can develop more effective incident response strategies. Knowing which stage an attack is currently in can help teams prioritize their actions, allocate resources efficiently, and respond more effectively to minimize damage.

**Resource Allocation**: The framework helps organizations allocate resources more effectively by identifying critical points within their systems that require enhanced security measures. This targeted approach can lead to more efficient use of security budgets and personnel.

The Cyber Kill Chain is a vital tool for understanding the lifecycle of cyberattacks, providing a structured framework for detecting, preventing, and responding to threats. By familiarizing themselves with each stage of the kill chain, organizations can implement targeted defenses and develop comprehensive incident response strategies that mitigate risks and enhance their overall security posture.

As cyber threats continue to evolve, understanding the intricacies of the Cyber Kill Chain will remain essential for organizations striving to protect their digital assets and respond effectively to an increasingly complex threat landscape. By adopting a proactive mindset and leveraging the insights provided by the Cyber Kill Chain, organizations can better safeguard themselves against the persistent and adaptive nature of modern cybercrime.

## 2.2 The MITRE ATT&CK Framework: A Comprehensive Guide

In the ever-evolving landscape of cybersecurity, organizations face an increasing number of sophisticated cyber threats. To effectively defend against these threats, it is crucial to understand the tactics, techniques, and procedures (TTPs) used by adversaries. The MITRE ATT&CK framework provides a comprehensive and systematic approach to this understanding, serving as a valuable resource for threat intelligence, defense strategies, and incident response. This chapter explores the key components of the MITRE ATT&CK framework and its significance in enhancing cybersecurity measures.

### Overview of the MITRE ATT&CK Framework

The MITRE ATT&CK framework (Adversarial Tactics, Techniques, and Common Knowledge) is a living knowledge base that catalogs and describes the behaviors and methods employed by cyber adversaries. Developed by MITRE Corporation, ATT&CK is based on real-world observations of cyberattacks and is continuously updated to reflect the evolving threat landscape. The framework is designed to be comprehensive, covering a wide array of tactics and techniques across various platforms, including Windows, macOS, Linux, mobile devices, and cloud environments.

### Key Components

**Tactics**: Tactics represent the overarching goals that adversaries aim to achieve during an attack. Each tactic corresponds to a specific phase of the attack lifecycle, such as initial access, execution, persistence, privilege escalation, and exfiltration. Understanding these tactics helps security teams identify the objectives behind adversary behavior.

**Techniques**: Techniques are the specific methods employed by adversaries to achieve their tactical goals. Each technique provides a detailed description of how an attack can be carried out, including relevant examples and potential indicators of compromise (IOCs). Techniques may have multiple variations, reflecting different ways adversaries can implement a particular method.

**Sub-techniques**: In addition to techniques, ATT&CK also defines sub-techniques, which offer a more granular view of how specific techniques can be executed. This level of detail helps organizations understand the nuances of adversary behavior and tailor their defenses accordingly.

**Procedures**: Procedures are the specific implementations of techniques used by adversaries in real-world attacks. These are often based on documented cases of cyber incidents and provide valuable context for security teams, enabling them to recognize patterns and potential threats.

**Mitigations**: For each technique, the ATT&CK framework provides suggested mitigations and defenses that organizations can implement to reduce the likelihood of successful attacks. This proactive approach empowers security teams to develop comprehensive security strategies.

**Detection**: The framework also includes guidance on detection strategies for each technique. By understanding what to look for, security teams can enhance their monitoring and threat detection capabilities, allowing for quicker identification of adversarial activities.

## Structure of the MITRE ATT&CK Framework

The MITRE ATT&CK framework is organized into matrices that categorize tactics and techniques according to various platforms:

**Enterprise Matrix**: Covers tactics and techniques applicable to enterprise environments, focusing on Windows, macOS, and Linux systems.

**Mobile Matrix**: Addresses tactics and techniques relevant to mobile devices, including iOS and Android platforms.

**Cloud Matrix**: Focuses on tactics and techniques used in cloud environments, reflecting the unique challenges and security considerations associated with cloud computing.

Each matrix provides a visual representation of the relationship between tactics and techniques, enabling security professionals to easily identify relevant threats and associated defensive measures.

## Importance of the MITRE ATT&CK Framework

The MITRE ATT&CK framework offers several key benefits for organizations seeking to enhance their cybersecurity posture:

**Threat Intelligence**: By mapping real-world adversary behavior, ATT&CK provides valuable insights into the TTPs used by cybercriminals. This information helps organizations better understand the threats they face and prioritize their security efforts accordingly.

**Incident Response**: The framework serves as a guide for incident response teams, helping them to recognize and respond to specific attack techniques. By understanding the tactics and techniques associated with an incident, teams can develop targeted response strategies to mitigate damage.

**Security Assessment**: Organizations can use the ATT&CK framework to assess their current security measures against known adversary techniques. This assessment can identify gaps in defenses and inform security improvement initiatives.

**Threat Hunting**: The framework supports proactive threat hunting efforts by providing a structured approach for security teams to search for indicators of compromise related to specific techniques. This helps identify potential threats before they can cause significant harm.

**Training and Awareness**: The ATT&CK framework is a valuable resource for training security personnel and raising awareness of cyber threats. By familiarizing staff with the framework, organizations can improve their overall security culture and readiness.

**Practical Application of the MITRE ATT&CK Framework**

Organizations can implement the MITRE ATT&CK framework in several ways to enhance their cybersecurity efforts:

**Mapping Security Controls**: Organizations can map their existing security controls to the ATT&CK techniques to evaluate the effectiveness of their defenses. This mapping can inform security improvements and help ensure that critical techniques are adequately addressed.

**Creating Threat Models**: Security teams can use the framework to develop threat models based on the tactics and techniques relevant to their organization. These models can guide security planning and resource allocation.

**Conducting Red Team Exercises**: Red teams can leverage the ATT&CK framework to simulate adversary behavior during penetration testing and red team exercises. This approach helps organizations identify vulnerabilities and improve their defenses based on real-world scenarios.

**Integrating with SIEM Solutions**: Security Information and Event Management (SIEM) solutions can integrate ATT&CK knowledge to enhance threat detection capabilities. By correlating alerts with known techniques, organizations can improve the accuracy and relevance of their security monitoring.

**Challenges and Limitations**

While the MITRE ATT&CK framework is a powerful tool for understanding cyber threats, it does have some limitations:

**Complexity**: The breadth and depth of the ATT&CK framework can be overwhelming for some organizations, especially smaller ones with limited cybersecurity resources. Prioritizing which techniques to address first may require careful consideration.

**Dynamic Threat Landscape**: The cyber threat landscape is continually evolving, and while the ATT&CK framework is regularly updated, there may be emerging techniques that are not yet documented. Organizations must remain vigilant and stay informed about new threats.

**False Sense of Security**: Relying solely on the ATT&CK framework without implementing other cybersecurity best practices can create a false sense of security. Organizations should adopt a holistic approach to cybersecurity, integrating various frameworks and practices to achieve comprehensive protection.

The MITRE ATT&CK framework is an invaluable resource for understanding and mitigating cyber threats in today's digital landscape. By providing a structured approach to analyzing adversary tactics, techniques, and procedures, ATT&CK empowers organizations to improve their threat detection, incident response, and overall cybersecurity posture.

As the cyber threat landscape continues to evolve, leveraging the insights offered by the MITRE ATT&CK framework will be essential for organizations striving to protect their digital assets and respond effectively to emerging challenges. By adopting a proactive mindset and utilizing the framework as a foundational tool in their cybersecurity efforts, organizations can enhance their resilience against the ever-present threats posed by cyber adversaries.

## 2.3 Using Frameworks for Threat Intelligence and Prevention

In the complex and constantly evolving landscape of cybersecurity, frameworks play a crucial role in enhancing threat intelligence and prevention strategies. By providing structured methodologies for understanding threats, analyzing vulnerabilities, and formulating responses, these frameworks empower organizations to proactively defend against cyberattacks. This chapter explores how various frameworks, including the MITRE ATT&CK, Cyber Kill Chain, and others, can be effectively utilized for threat intelligence and prevention.

**The Role of Frameworks in Cybersecurity**

Frameworks serve as foundational tools that offer a systematic approach to understanding and mitigating cybersecurity threats. They help organizations:

**Standardize Terminology**: Frameworks create a common language for discussing cybersecurity concepts, facilitating communication between technical and non-technical stakeholders.

**Organize Threat Information**: By categorizing threats into identifiable components, frameworks enable security teams to analyze and prioritize risks effectively.

**Enhance Collaboration**: Frameworks promote collaboration across teams and departments, fostering a more cohesive approach to threat intelligence and prevention.

**Guide Security Practices**: Frameworks provide guidelines and best practices for implementing effective security measures, helping organizations build robust defenses against threats.

**Key Frameworks for Threat Intelligence and Prevention**

MITRE ATT&CK Framework: As discussed in the previous section, the MITRE ATT&CK framework provides a comprehensive catalog of adversary tactics, techniques, and procedures (TTPs). By mapping threats to this framework, organizations can:

- **Identify Vulnerabilities**: Analyze which techniques are relevant to their environment and identify areas where defenses may be weak or absent.
- **Develop Threat Intelligence**: Use ATT&CK to inform threat intelligence efforts by correlating observed adversary behaviors with known techniques, enhancing situational awareness.
- **Prioritize Defenses**: Focus resources on defending against techniques that are most likely to be used against them, ensuring a targeted approach to cybersecurity.

**Cyber Kill Chain**: The Cyber Kill Chain framework outlines the phases of a cyberattack, providing insights into the adversary's lifecycle. Organizations can leverage this framework to:

- **Implement Prevention Measures**: Understand the stages of an attack enables teams to implement preventive measures at each phase, such as improving email security to block phishing attempts during the delivery phase.
- **Enhance Incident Response**: By recognizing which stage of the kill chain an attack is in, incident response teams can allocate resources effectively and develop targeted response strategies to mitigate the impact.

**NIST Cybersecurity Framework**: The National Institute of Standards and Technology (NIST) Cybersecurity Framework is a voluntary framework that provides guidelines for managing cybersecurity risks. Its core functions—Identify, Protect, Detect, Respond, and Recover—help organizations develop comprehensive security strategies. Key applications include:

- **Risk Assessment**: Organizations can assess their current cybersecurity posture and identify gaps based on the framework's guidelines.
- **Security Control Implementation**: The framework guides organizations in implementing security controls tailored to their risk profile, enhancing overall resilience.

**Lockheed Martin's Cyber Defense Matrix**: This framework visually represents the relationship between various security controls and stages of the cyber kill chain. Organizations can use it to:

- **Map Security Controls**: Align security technologies and practices with specific stages of an attack, ensuring comprehensive coverage of potential threats.
- **Identify Security Gaps**: Assess the effectiveness of existing controls and identify areas where additional measures are needed to enhance threat prevention.

**Integrating Frameworks into Threat Intelligence Programs**

To maximize the effectiveness of frameworks in threat intelligence and prevention, organizations should consider the following best practices:

**Establish a Threat Intelligence Program**: Create a formal program that incorporates various frameworks into daily operations. This includes assigning dedicated resources, establishing processes for intelligence gathering, and ensuring collaboration between teams.

**Continuous Monitoring and Analysis**: Employ continuous monitoring to collect data on potential threats and vulnerabilities. Regularly analyze this data against the frameworks to identify trends, emerging threats, and areas for improvement.

**Training and Awareness**: Educate employees on the significance of these frameworks and their role in threat intelligence and prevention. Training programs should focus on how to recognize and respond to potential threats, fostering a security-conscious culture within the organization.

**Collaboration with External Sources**: Engage with industry partners, threat intelligence sharing platforms, and law enforcement agencies to gain insights into emerging threats. By leveraging external intelligence, organizations can enhance their understanding of the threat landscape and adapt their defenses accordingly.

**Regular Updates and Reviews**: Cyber threats are dynamic, necessitating regular reviews and updates of security measures and frameworks. Organizations should stay informed about changes in the threat landscape and adjust their strategies based on the latest intelligence and framework updates.

**Utilizing Frameworks for Incident Response**

Frameworks can significantly enhance an organization's incident response capabilities:

**Incident Detection**: By mapping incidents to specific techniques within frameworks like MITRE ATT&CK, organizations can improve their detection capabilities. This enables security teams to identify signs of compromise more quickly and accurately.

**Response Playbooks**: Develop response playbooks based on the frameworks, outlining specific actions to take for each identified tactic or technique. These playbooks should include escalation procedures, communication protocols, and post-incident analysis steps.

**Lessons Learned**: After an incident, organizations should conduct post-mortem analyses to evaluate how well their frameworks guided their response. This review should identify strengths and weaknesses, informing future prevention and response strategies.

Utilizing frameworks for threat intelligence and prevention is essential for organizations navigating the complex cybersecurity landscape. By leveraging frameworks like MITRE ATT&CK, the Cyber Kill Chain, the NIST Cybersecurity Framework, and others, organizations can develop a systematic approach to understanding and mitigating cyber threats.

Through effective implementation of these frameworks, organizations can enhance their threat intelligence capabilities, strengthen their security posture, and improve their incident response strategies. As cyber threats continue to evolve, a proactive and framework-driven approach will be critical for organizations seeking to protect their digital assets and maintain resilience in the face of adversity. By fostering a culture of continuous learning and adaptation, organizations can stay one step ahead of cyber adversaries and safeguard their operations in an increasingly digital world.

# Chapter 3: Digital Forensics Fundamentals

In this chapter, we lay the groundwork for understanding digital forensics, a critical discipline in the fight against cybercrime. We will define key concepts and terminology essential to the field, explore the types of digital evidence that can be collected—from hard drives to cloud storage—and discuss the various methodologies employed throughout the forensic process. Emphasizing the importance of a meticulous and methodical approach, this chapter will guide readers through the steps involved in conducting a digital forensic investigation, from initial evidence collection to final analysis. By grasping these foundational principles, readers will be better equipped to recognize the value of digital forensics in uncovering hidden truths and supporting legal proceedings in the digital age.

## 3.1 Key Concepts in Digital Forensics

Digital forensics is a critical discipline within cybersecurity that focuses on the identification, preservation, analysis, and presentation of data found on digital devices. As the prevalence of digital technology continues to rise, so does the need for effective forensic practices to investigate cybercrime, data breaches, and other digital incidents. This chapter outlines the key concepts in digital forensics that serve as the foundation for conducting thorough investigations and understanding the complexities of digital evidence.

**1. Digital Evidence**

Digital evidence refers to any data stored or transmitted in digital form that can be used in a legal context. This evidence can originate from a variety of sources, including:

- **Computers**: Hard drives, SSDs, and system memory (RAM) can store a wealth of information, such as files, emails, logs, and system configurations.
- **Mobile Devices**: Smartphones and tablets often contain text messages, call logs, application data, and geolocation information that may be relevant to investigations.
- **Network Devices**: Routers, switches, and firewalls can provide logs and metadata that help trace network activity and identify malicious behavior.
- **Cloud Services**: Data stored in cloud environments can include emails, documents, and other digital artifacts that may be critical in forensic investigations.

The primary challenge in handling digital evidence is ensuring its integrity and authenticity, as any alterations can compromise its admissibility in legal proceedings.

## 2. Chain of Custody

The chain of custody is a critical concept in digital forensics that refers to the process of maintaining and documenting the handling of evidence from the moment it is collected until it is presented in court. A proper chain of custody ensures that:

- **Evidence is Preserved**: Maintaining the original condition of the evidence prevents tampering, contamination, or loss of data.
- **Accountability**: Each person who handles the evidence must be documented, establishing accountability and credibility.
- **Legal Admissibility**: Courts require clear evidence of the chain of custody to accept digital evidence as admissible, demonstrating that it has not been altered or compromised.

To establish a proper chain of custody, forensic investigators should use standardized procedures for collecting, storing, and documenting evidence, including using evidence bags, sealing methods, and logging all actions taken.

## 3. Forensic Imaging

Forensic imaging is the process of creating an exact bit-for-bit copy of a digital storage device, such as a hard drive or memory card. This copy, known as a forensic image, is crucial for several reasons:

- **Preservation of Original Data**: Investigators work with the forensic image instead of the original device, preserving the integrity of the original data.
- **Comprehensive Analysis**: A forensic image allows investigators to analyze the entire contents of a device, including deleted files and unallocated space, which can contain valuable evidence.
- **Reproducibility**: The ability to create multiple forensic images enables other investigators to verify findings and conduct independent analyses.

Forensic imaging typically involves specialized software tools that ensure the process is thorough and that the image accurately reflects the data on the original device.

## 4. Analysis Techniques

Digital forensic analysis involves a variety of techniques and tools to extract and interpret data from forensic images and other digital evidence. Common analysis techniques include:

- **File Recovery**: Techniques to recover deleted files from a storage medium, which may involve examining file system structures and using software to reconstruct lost data.
- **Keyword Searches**: Searching for specific terms or phrases within files and metadata to uncover relevant information related to an investigation.
- **Timeline Analysis**: Creating timelines of events based on timestamps from file modifications, access logs, and other data to understand the sequence of actions taken on a device.
- **Artifact Analysis**: Investigating specific artifacts, such as browser history, registry entries, and system logs, to gather evidence about user behavior and system interactions.

Each of these techniques plays a crucial role in uncovering the context surrounding an incident and identifying potential suspects or malicious activities.

## 5. Reporting and Presentation

Once the analysis is complete, the findings must be documented in a clear and organized manner. The reporting phase of digital forensics involves:

- **Creating a Forensic Report**: A detailed document that outlines the methods used, evidence collected, findings, and conclusions drawn from the analysis. This report serves as a vital piece of documentation for legal proceedings.
- **Presenting Evidence**: Forensic investigators may need to present their findings in court or to stakeholders, requiring the ability to communicate complex technical information in an understandable manner.
- **Expert Testimony**: In some cases, digital forensic experts may be called to testify in court, explaining the methods used and the implications of the findings.

Effective reporting and presentation are critical to ensuring that the evidence is understood and accepted by legal authorities and can influence the outcome of investigations and trials.

## 6. Legal and Ethical Considerations

Digital forensics is not only a technical discipline but also one that operates within a legal and ethical framework. Key legal and ethical considerations include:

- **Compliance with Laws**: Investigators must be aware of applicable laws and regulations related to privacy, data protection, and evidence handling to ensure compliance during investigations.
- **Informed Consent**: Obtaining consent from individuals before accessing their devices or data is critical to maintaining ethical standards and legal compliance.
- **Bias and Objectivity**: Forensic investigators must remain objective and impartial, ensuring that their analyses are not influenced by personal beliefs or external pressures.

Understanding the legal and ethical landscape surrounding digital forensics is essential for maintaining the integrity of investigations and ensuring that findings are credible and admissible in court.

The field of digital forensics is a complex and dynamic area of study that requires a solid understanding of key concepts, practices, and legal considerations. By mastering these foundational principles—such as digital evidence, chain of custody, forensic imaging, analysis techniques, reporting, and ethical considerations—investigators can conduct thorough and effective investigations into cyber incidents.

As technology continues to evolve, so too will the practices and challenges of digital forensics. Therefore, continuous learning and adaptation will be essential for forensic professionals seeking to stay ahead in this critical field. By leveraging these key concepts, organizations and investigators can enhance their ability to uncover, analyze, and present digital evidence, ultimately contributing to the fight against cybercrime and ensuring justice in the digital realm.

## 3.2 Types of Digital Evidence: An Overview

Digital evidence plays a crucial role in the investigation of cybercrime, data breaches, and various other legal matters. It encompasses a wide array of information that can be collected from electronic devices, digital communications, and online activities. Understanding the different types of digital evidence is essential for forensic investigators, law enforcement, and cybersecurity professionals. This chapter provides an overview of the various categories of digital evidence, their characteristics, and their relevance in forensic investigations.

## 1. Computer-Based Evidence

Computer-based evidence is one of the most common forms of digital evidence encountered in forensic investigations. This type includes data stored on personal computers, laptops, and servers. Key components include:

**File Systems**: Investigators analyze file structures, directories, and metadata to gather information about user activity, file access, and modifications. Important files may include documents, spreadsheets, presentations, and images.

**Operating System Artifacts**: The operating system generates numerous logs and artifacts that provide insights into user behavior and system activity. These include system logs, application logs, and user activity logs that can reveal when and how a system was accessed or altered.

**User Accounts**: Information about user accounts, including login credentials, user permissions, and account activity, can be critical in understanding unauthorized access or user actions on a system.

**Temporary Files and Cache**: Temporary files, cache data, and other remnants of user activity can contain evidence of past actions, even if the user has deleted other files.

## 2. Mobile Device Evidence

With the widespread use of smartphones and tablets, mobile devices have become significant sources of digital evidence. Mobile device evidence includes:

**Text Messages and Call Logs**: SMS and MMS messages, as well as call logs, can provide direct communication evidence, including dates, times, participants, and the content of messages.

**Application Data**: Mobile applications can store various types of data, including social media interactions, GPS location data, and user-generated content. Forensic analysis can reveal how and when apps were used.

**Geolocation Data**: Many mobile devices have GPS capabilities, and the geolocation data can provide crucial evidence about a user's location at specific times. This information can be used to establish alibis or connections to criminal activity.

**Email and Contacts**: Emails stored on mobile devices can provide critical insights into communications and relationships, while contact lists can help establish connections between individuals.

### 3. Network-Based Evidence

Network-based evidence refers to data collected from network devices and communications. This type of evidence is essential for understanding the flow of information and identifying unauthorized access or malicious activities. Key components include:

**Network Logs**: Routers, switches, and firewalls generate logs that document network traffic, connection attempts, and access patterns. Analyzing these logs can help identify suspicious activities or breaches.

**Intrusion Detection Systems (IDS) Data**: IDS tools monitor network traffic for suspicious activities and can provide alerts and logs detailing potential intrusions.

**Traffic Analysis**: Capturing and analyzing network traffic can reveal the types of communications occurring, including data transfers, protocols used, and destinations contacted.

**VPN and Proxy Logs**: Virtual Private Networks (VPNs) and proxy servers often log user connections, helping investigators trace user activities that may have been masked or obscured.

### 4. Cloud-Based Evidence

As organizations increasingly rely on cloud computing services, cloud-based evidence has become essential in investigations. This type of evidence includes:

**Stored Data**: Files, documents, and databases stored in cloud services can provide evidence about business activities, communications, and transactions.

**Access Logs**: Cloud service providers maintain logs of user access and activity, which can show when and how users interacted with the cloud environment.

**Collaboration Tools**: Many organizations use cloud-based collaboration tools (e.g., Google Workspace, Microsoft 365) that may store emails, chat histories, and version histories of documents.

**Backup Data**: Cloud backup services may retain historical data that can be invaluable for recovering deleted or lost information relevant to an investigation.

## 5. Email Evidence

Email communications are critical pieces of digital evidence in many investigations, especially those related to fraud, harassment, or conspiracy. Key elements include:

**Email Headers**: Email headers contain metadata about the email, such as the sender, recipient, subject line, timestamps, and routing information. Analyzing headers can reveal the path taken by the email and identify potential spoofing or forging.

**Content of Emails**: The body of emails can contain valuable information, including attachments, links, and discussions about sensitive topics or criminal activity.

**Email Accounts**: Information about email account settings, security features, and access history can provide context for the investigation and help establish user intent.

## 6. Social Media Evidence

Social media platforms generate a vast amount of data that can be instrumental in investigations. This type of evidence includes:

**Posts and Comments**: Public and private posts, comments, and interactions can provide insights into user behavior, relationships, and intentions.

**Photos and Videos**: Multimedia content shared on social media can serve as evidence of activities, locations, or events that may be relevant to an investigation.

**Profiles and Connections**: User profiles often contain personal information, relationships, and social networks that can help establish connections between individuals.

**Direct Messages**: Private messages exchanged on social media can contain conversations that may be relevant to the investigation.

## 7. Internet of Things (IoT) Evidence

As IoT devices become more prevalent, the data generated by these devices can be relevant in various investigations. IoT evidence includes:

**Device Logs**: Many IoT devices, such as smart home appliances and wearables, generate logs that track their operation and interactions. These logs can provide insights into user activities and device usage patterns.

**Sensor Data**: IoT devices equipped with sensors can provide valuable data, such as environmental conditions, movements, and other activity metrics that may be relevant in investigations.

**Connectivity Data**: Information about how IoT devices connect to networks can help investigators understand their role in an incident or identify unauthorized access.

**8. Physical Evidence Related to Digital Evidence**

In some cases, physical evidence may be linked to digital evidence. This includes:

**Storage Media**: Physical devices such as hard drives, USB drives, and memory cards that store digital evidence can provide direct access to the data needed for investigation.

**Device Seizures**: Physical possession of devices can allow investigators to conduct forensic examinations and extract digital evidence from them.

**Documentation**: Manuals, receipts, or other paperwork that accompany devices can provide context about ownership, usage, or transactions related to the evidence.

Digital evidence encompasses a diverse array of information derived from various electronic devices and digital activities. Understanding the different types of digital evidence is essential for forensic investigators, law enforcement officials, and cybersecurity professionals as they navigate the complexities of cybercrime investigations.

By recognizing the significance of computer-based evidence, mobile device evidence, network-based evidence, cloud-based evidence, email evidence, social media evidence, IoT evidence, and the interplay between physical and digital evidence, investigators can adopt a comprehensive approach to uncovering the truth in digital investigations. As technology continues to evolve, the ability to effectively identify, analyze, and present digital evidence will remain a cornerstone of successful forensic practices in the fight against cybercrime.

## 3.3 The Forensic Process: Steps from Collection to Analysis

Digital forensics is a meticulous and systematic process that involves multiple steps, from the initial collection of digital evidence to its analysis and presentation in a court of law. Each step is critical to ensuring that the evidence is collected, preserved, and analyzed in a manner that maintains its integrity and admissibility. This chapter outlines the forensic process, detailing the key steps involved in digital investigations.

**1. Preparation**

The forensic process begins long before any evidence is collected. Preparation involves:

**Establishing Policies and Procedures**: Organizations must have clear guidelines in place for handling digital evidence. These procedures should outline the roles and responsibilities of personnel involved in digital investigations.

**Training Personnel**: Forensic investigators and IT staff should receive training on forensic techniques, legal considerations, and the tools required for evidence collection and analysis.

**Creating a Response Plan**: Organizations should develop incident response plans that outline how to react to various types of incidents, including cyberattacks, data breaches, or insider threats. This includes identifying key personnel, communication protocols, and escalation procedures.

**2. Identification**

The next step is to identify potential sources of digital evidence. This involves:

**Determining Scope**: Investigators must establish the scope of the investigation, determining which devices, systems, and data sources may contain relevant evidence.

**Identifying Relevant Devices**: Potential sources may include computers, mobile devices, servers, cloud storage, network devices, and even IoT devices. Understanding where evidence is likely to be found is crucial for efficient collection.

**Gathering Contextual Information**: Collecting contextual information about the incident is essential for understanding the environment in which the evidence exists. This includes identifying users, system configurations, and relevant activities that may be linked to the investigation.

## 3. Collection

The collection phase is critical for ensuring that digital evidence is gathered in a forensically sound manner. Key activities include:

**Using Proper Tools**: Forensic investigators utilize specialized tools and software for data acquisition. These tools are designed to create exact bit-by-bit copies of digital storage devices without altering the original data.

**Documenting the Process**: Every action taken during the collection process must be meticulously documented. This includes details about the devices accessed, the methods used for collection, and the personnel involved.

**Maintaining Chain of Custody**: The chain of custody must be established and maintained throughout the collection process. This involves labeling and securing the evidence, along with recording all transfers and handling of the evidence to ensure its integrity.

**Collecting Volatile Data**: Investigators should prioritize collecting volatile data (e.g., RAM contents, running processes) that may be lost during system shutdowns or reboots. This data can be critical for understanding the state of the system at the time of the incident.

## 4. Preservation

Preserving digital evidence is essential to prevent alteration or degradation. This step includes:

**Creating Forensic Images**: After collecting evidence, investigators create forensic images of the original data. These images are exact copies that can be used for analysis while preserving the original data in its unaltered state.

**Storing Evidence Securely**: All collected evidence must be stored in a secure environment, protected from unauthorized access, environmental hazards, or physical damage. Access controls and environmental monitoring may be implemented to safeguard the evidence.

**Verifying Integrity**: Investigators should use cryptographic hashing (e.g., MD5, SHA-256) to create hash values for the original evidence and the forensic images. This verification process ensures that the evidence remains unchanged throughout the investigation.

## 5. Analysis

The analysis phase is where investigators examine the collected evidence to uncover relevant information. This step involves:

**Data Processing**: Forensic tools process the collected data to extract meaningful information, such as files, email communications, user activity logs, and more.

**Examination of Artifacts**: Investigators examine specific artifacts, including file systems, application logs, and registry entries, to reconstruct user actions and identify anomalies.

**Keyword Searches and Data Mining**: Investigators may perform keyword searches to identify relevant content and conduct data mining techniques to discover patterns or connections that may indicate malicious activity.

**Timeline Creation**: Constructing a timeline of events based on timestamps from files, logs, and other data helps investigators understand the sequence of actions taken and identify key moments in the investigation.

**Correlation of Evidence**: Analysts correlate findings across different sources of evidence to build a comprehensive understanding of the incident, linking user behavior to specific actions and uncovering the broader context.

## 6. Reporting

Once the analysis is complete, investigators must prepare a comprehensive report that outlines their findings. Key elements of reporting include:

**Documentation of Methods**: The report should detail the methodologies used for evidence collection and analysis, including tools and techniques applied throughout the investigation.

**Findings and Conclusions**: Clearly articulate the findings of the investigation, presenting relevant evidence and drawing conclusions based on the analysis conducted.

**Visual Aids**: Including visual aids such as charts, timelines, and graphs can help convey complex information in an easily understandable format.

**Recommendations**: If applicable, the report should include recommendations for improving security practices, preventing future incidents, or addressing vulnerabilities identified during the investigation.

## 7. Presentation

The final step in the forensic process is the presentation of findings. This may occur in various contexts:

**Internal Stakeholders**: Investigators may present their findings to organizational leadership or relevant teams, providing insights into the incident and recommending actions to mitigate risks.

**Legal Proceedings**: If the case leads to legal action, forensic investigators may be called upon to testify in court. They must be prepared to explain their methodologies, findings, and the significance of the evidence in a clear and concise manner.

**Expert Testimony**: Forensic experts must present complex technical information to a non-technical audience, ensuring that their findings are understood by judges, juries, and legal professionals.

The forensic process is a systematic approach to investigating digital incidents, encompassing preparation, identification, collection, preservation, analysis, reporting, and presentation. Each step plays a crucial role in ensuring that digital evidence is handled properly and that findings are credible and admissible in legal contexts.

By following these steps diligently and maintaining the integrity of the evidence throughout the process, forensic investigators can provide valuable insights into cyber incidents, support legal proceedings, and contribute to the broader field of cybersecurity. As technology continues to evolve, mastering the forensic process will remain essential for addressing the challenges posed by digital crimes and ensuring justice in the digital age.

# Chapter 4: Collecting Evidence: Tools and Techniques

In this chapter, we focus on the critical processes involved in collecting digital evidence, equipping readers with the tools and techniques necessary for effective evidence acquisition. We will explore a variety of digital imaging techniques that ensure the integrity of data, as well as the specialized software and hardware tools available for data recovery and analysis. Emphasizing the importance of maintaining the chain of custody, we will outline best practices for documenting the collection process to ensure that evidence is admissible in court. By the end of this chapter, readers will have a comprehensive understanding of how to gather digital evidence systematically and ethically, laying the foundation for successful cybercrime investigations.

## 4.1 Digital Imaging Techniques: Preserving Evidence

Digital imaging techniques are essential for the collection and preservation of digital evidence in forensic investigations. These techniques ensure that data from digital devices is accurately captured and retained in a manner that maintains its integrity and authenticity. In this section, we will explore the various digital imaging methods used in forensic practice, the importance of these techniques in preserving evidence, and best practices for effective imaging.

### 1. Understanding Digital Imaging

Digital imaging refers to the process of creating a bit-for-bit copy of data stored on a digital medium. This includes not only the visible files but also deleted data, system files, and unallocated space. The primary objective of digital imaging is to preserve the original evidence while allowing investigators to analyze the duplicate without altering the original data.

Digital imaging techniques are critical in maintaining the chain of custody, ensuring that the evidence remains admissible in court. Proper imaging techniques also enable forensic analysts to conduct thorough investigations by providing a comprehensive view of the data available on the original device.

### 2. Types of Digital Imaging Techniques

Several methods can be employed to create forensic images of digital devices. The choice of technique often depends on the type of device, the nature of the investigation, and the specific requirements of the forensic analysis.

**Physical Imaging:**

Physical imaging involves creating a complete copy of the entire storage device, including all data, file systems, and unallocated space. This technique captures every bit of information on the medium, providing a comprehensive representation of the data.

Tools such as FTK Imager and EnCase are commonly used for physical imaging. They allow investigators to create an exact duplicate of hard drives, SSDs, and other storage devices.

**Logical Imaging:**

Logical imaging focuses on specific files or folders rather than capturing the entire storage medium. This technique is often used when investigators are only interested in certain data sets, such as documents, images, or emails.

Logical imaging can be accomplished using tools like WinHex and X1 Search, which enable investigators to extract and analyze specific data without needing to image the entire device.

**Live Imaging:**

Live imaging is performed while the device is still powered on and operational. This technique is particularly useful for collecting volatile data such as RAM contents, running processes, and network connections that would otherwise be lost if the device were turned off.

Tools like FTK Imager and Live Response are often used for live imaging. However, it is crucial to take precautions to avoid altering data during the imaging process.

**Memory Imaging:**

Memory imaging specifically targets the contents of a computer's RAM. This type of imaging captures active processes, network connections, and temporary files that can provide valuable evidence about system activity at a specific point in time.

Tools like Volatility and Memoryze can be employed to capture and analyze memory images, providing insights into potential malware or unauthorized access.

## 3. Best Practices for Digital Imaging

To ensure that digital imaging is performed effectively and preserves the integrity of the evidence, forensic investigators should follow established best practices:

**Use Forensically Sound Tools**: Always use industry-recognized forensic imaging tools that are designed for data acquisition. These tools should be capable of creating exact copies of data while preserving its integrity.

**Verify Hash Values**: Before and after imaging, investigators should generate cryptographic hash values (e.g., MD5, SHA-256) for the original evidence and the forensic image. Hash values provide a way to verify that the data has not been altered during the imaging process.

**Document Every Step**: Meticulously document all actions taken during the imaging process, including the tools used, timestamps, and personnel involved. This documentation forms part of the chain of custody and is critical for maintaining the credibility of the evidence.

**Secure the Original Evidence**: Once imaging is complete, the original device should be stored securely to prevent unauthorized access or tampering. Use evidence bags, locks, or tamper-evident seals to safeguard the original evidence.

**Create Multiple Copies**: If possible, create multiple forensic images to ensure redundancy. This allows for independent analysis and reduces the risk of data loss during investigations.

## 4. Challenges in Digital Imaging

While digital imaging is a fundamental aspect of digital forensics, several challenges can arise:

**Device Encryption**: Many modern devices employ encryption to protect data. Forensic investigators may need specialized tools and techniques to bypass or decrypt this data without compromising evidence integrity.

**Volatile Data Loss**: Data residing in RAM is temporary and may be lost if the device is powered off or rebooted. Investigators must prioritize live imaging when dealing with devices containing volatile data.

**Damaged or Corrupted Media**: Physical damage or corruption of storage media can hinder the imaging process. In such cases, forensic specialists may need to use specialized recovery tools and techniques to retrieve data.

**5. Legal Considerations**

Digital imaging must comply with legal and ethical standards to ensure the admissibility of evidence in court. Key legal considerations include:

**Consent**: Investigators must obtain proper consent before accessing and imaging devices, especially in private settings. Failure to obtain consent can lead to legal repercussions and the inadmissibility of evidence.

**Chain of Custody**: Maintaining a clear and documented chain of custody is crucial for demonstrating the integrity of the evidence. This includes recording every transfer, handling, and access to the evidence throughout the imaging process.

**Adherence to Regulations**: Investigators should be aware of and comply with relevant laws and regulations governing data privacy, protection, and evidence handling in their jurisdiction.

Digital imaging techniques are vital for preserving evidence in forensic investigations. By employing proper imaging methods, adhering to best practices, and navigating the legal landscape, forensic investigators can ensure the integrity and admissibility of digital evidence. As technology continues to advance and new challenges arise, ongoing education and adaptation of imaging techniques will be essential for effective digital forensics in an ever-evolving digital landscape.

## 4.2 Data Recovery Tools: Finding Deleted Files

Data recovery is a critical aspect of digital forensics that involves retrieving lost, deleted, or corrupted files from various storage devices. In many investigations, deleted files can provide vital evidence regarding user activities, communications, and potential wrongdoing. This chapter explores the various data recovery tools available to forensic investigators, how these tools work, and best practices for their use in finding deleted files.

**1. Understanding Data Deletion**

Before delving into the tools, it's important to understand how data deletion occurs on digital devices. When a user deletes a file, the operating system typically does not erase the file's data immediately. Instead, it marks the space occupied by the file as available for new data, allowing the operating system to overwrite it later. This means that as long as the deleted file's data has not been overwritten, there is a possibility of recovery.

**2. Types of Data Recovery Tools**

There are various data recovery tools designed to help forensic investigators retrieve deleted files. These tools vary in complexity, functionality, and cost. Here are some of the most commonly used categories of data recovery tools:

**File Carving Tools:**

- File carving is a technique used to recover files based on their content rather than their file system metadata. This method is particularly useful for recovering files that have been deleted or corrupted, as it bypasses the need for intact file system structures.
- Tools like Scalpel and Foremost are popular choices for file carving. They analyze disk images and look for file signatures to reconstruct deleted files, regardless of their current status on the file system.

**File Recovery Software:**

- These are user-friendly applications designed for general data recovery tasks. They often have graphical user interfaces and can recover files from various storage media, including hard drives, USB drives, and memory cards.
- Examples include Recuva, EaseUS Data Recovery Wizard, and Disk Drill. These tools typically offer wizards to guide users through the recovery process, making them accessible even to non-technical users.

**Forensic Recovery Tools:**

- Forensic recovery tools are specialized applications designed specifically for digital investigations. They provide advanced features such as comprehensive analysis, hashing, and reporting capabilities.
- Tools like EnCase and FTK Imager not only facilitate data recovery but also integrate with the broader forensic workflow, including imaging and analysis of digital evidence.

**Disk Imaging Tools:**

- Before attempting recovery, it is best practice to create a forensic image of the original storage device. Imaging tools allow investigators to create an exact bit-for-bit copy of a drive, preserving the original data intact for analysis and recovery attempts.
- Tools such as dd (a command-line utility) and Acronis True Image are commonly used for this purpose.

### 3. How Data Recovery Tools Work

Data recovery tools utilize various techniques and algorithms to locate and recover deleted files. Here's a general overview of the recovery process:

**Scanning**: The recovery tool scans the storage medium for remnants of deleted files. This may involve a quick scan of the file system or a deep scan that examines the entire storage area, including unallocated space.

**File Signature Identification**: Many tools use file signatures—unique byte patterns that define different file types—to identify recoverable files. By matching these signatures against the data on the drive, the tool can reconstruct and recover files even if the file system entries are no longer present.

**Reconstruction**: Once a deleted file is identified, the recovery tool reconstructs the file, often restoring it to its original format. This process may involve piecing together fragmented files from different locations on the disk.

**Output and Verification**: After the recovery process, the tool presents the recovered files to the investigator. It is essential to verify the integrity of these files by checking their hashes against known values or using the files for intended analysis.

### 4. Best Practices for Using Data Recovery Tools

To maximize the chances of successful file recovery and maintain the integrity of the evidence, forensic investigators should adhere to the following best practices:

**Always Work on a Forensic Image**: Never attempt to recover files directly from the original storage device. Always create a forensic image first and perform recovery operations on this copy to prevent further data loss or alteration.

**Document the Recovery Process**: Maintain detailed documentation of every step taken during the recovery process, including the tools used, settings configured, and the rationale behind decisions. This documentation is critical for maintaining the chain of custody and ensuring the credibility of the findings.

**Choose the Right Tool**: Select the appropriate data recovery tool based on the specifics of the case, including the type of data lost, the storage medium involved, and the technical capabilities required. Different tools may yield varying results, so understanding their strengths and limitations is crucial.

**Conduct Controlled Recoveries**: In situations where multiple recovery attempts are possible, consider conducting controlled recoveries using different tools or settings. This approach can provide additional insights and potentially recover files that other tools could not.

**Verify Recovered Files**: After recovery, verify the integrity of the recovered files to ensure that they are complete and uncorrupted. This can be done by examining file properties, running hash comparisons, or opening files to check their contents.

## 5. Challenges in Data Recovery

While data recovery tools are powerful, they are not infallible. Several challenges can complicate the recovery process:

**Data Overwriting**: If new data has been written to the storage device since the files were deleted, recovery chances diminish significantly. The more time that passes and the more the device is used, the greater the likelihood that the deleted data will be overwritten.

**Encryption**: Files that have been encrypted present a significant challenge for recovery. Even if the underlying data is still intact, without the decryption keys, the recovered files may be unusable.

**Physical Damage**: Hard drives or storage devices that have suffered physical damage may not be recoverable through standard software methods. In such cases, specialized data recovery services may be required.

**Corrupted File Systems**: When file systems become corrupted, identifying the locations of deleted files can be more complicated. Recovery tools may struggle to interpret the data structures accurately.

### 6. Legal Considerations

Data recovery in the context of digital forensics must adhere to legal and ethical standards:

**Authorization**: Ensure that proper authorization has been obtained to recover data from the device in question. Unauthorized access can lead to legal consequences and render the recovered evidence inadmissible.

**Adherence to Procedures**: Follow established procedures for data recovery, particularly regarding documentation and evidence handling. This adherence is critical for maintaining the integrity of the investigation.

**Compliance with Data Protection Laws**: Investigators should be aware of and comply with data protection regulations and privacy laws, especially when dealing with personal data.

Data recovery tools are vital assets in the arsenal of digital forensic investigators, enabling them to retrieve deleted files and uncover crucial evidence. By understanding the various types of recovery tools, how they function, and best practices for their use, forensic professionals can maximize their chances of success in retrieving valuable information.

While challenges exist in the recovery process, adherence to established procedures and legal considerations will ensure that the recovered evidence remains reliable and admissible in court. As technology continues to evolve, staying informed about advancements in data recovery tools and techniques will be essential for effective digital investigations.

## 4.3 Maintaining Chain of Custody: Best Practices

In digital forensics, maintaining a clear and documented chain of custody is critical to ensuring the integrity and admissibility of digital evidence in legal proceedings. The chain of custody refers to the process of maintaining and documenting the handling of evidence from the moment it is collected until it is presented in court. This section outlines best practices for maintaining the chain of custody in digital investigations, emphasizing the importance of meticulous documentation, secure storage, and adherence to legal and ethical standards.

**1. Understanding Chain of Custody**

The chain of custody serves several essential functions in the context of digital forensics:

**Preservation of Evidence**: It ensures that the evidence remains intact and unaltered throughout the investigation process.

**Credibility**: A well-documented chain of custody lends credibility to the evidence, demonstrating that it has been handled appropriately and without tampering.

**Legal Admissibility**: Courts require a clear chain of custody to establish that evidence presented is authentic and has not been altered. A break in the chain can result in evidence being deemed inadmissible.

**2. Key Elements of Chain of Custody**

To maintain an effective chain of custody, investigators must focus on several key elements:

**Documentation**: Every action taken regarding the evidence must be documented thoroughly. This includes who collected the evidence, when it was collected, where it was stored, and any individuals who handled it thereafter.

**Labels and Identifiers**: Each piece of evidence should be labeled with a unique identifier, including a case number, description, date and time of collection, and the name of the individual who collected it. This information should be recorded in a chain of custody log.

**Secure Storage**: Evidence must be stored in a secure environment that prevents unauthorized access. This may involve using locked evidence bags, secure cabinets, or tamper-evident seals to protect the integrity of the evidence.

**Transfer Records**: Any time evidence is transferred from one person to another or from one location to another, a record must be made. This includes documenting the date and time of the transfer, the parties involved, and the condition of the evidence at the time of transfer.

## 3. Best Practices for Maintaining Chain of Custody

To effectively maintain the chain of custody, forensic investigators should implement the following best practices:

**Create a Chain of Custody Form**: Develop a standardized chain of custody form to capture all relevant information. This form should include fields for the case number, item description, collector's name, date and time of collection, and signatures from all individuals who handle the evidence.

**Use Forensically Sound Collection Methods**: When collecting digital evidence, use forensically sound methods that minimize the risk of alteration. This includes using appropriate imaging tools and techniques, as outlined in previous chapters.

**Secure Evidence Immediately**: Once evidence is collected, it should be secured immediately in a tamper-evident manner. This may involve sealing evidence bags or using locked evidence lockers to prevent unauthorized access.

**Implement Access Controls**: Restrict access to evidence storage areas to authorized personnel only. Use locks, security cameras, and electronic access controls to monitor who accesses the evidence.

**Regularly Review and Update Documentation**: Continuously update the chain of custody documentation as evidence changes hands or moves to different locations. Regularly review documentation for completeness and accuracy.

**Train Personnel**: Ensure that all personnel involved in handling evidence are trained on the importance of the chain of custody and the procedures required to maintain it. Ongoing training can help prevent unintentional breaches of custody.

## 4. Challenges in Maintaining Chain of Custody

Despite best efforts, several challenges can complicate the maintenance of the chain of custody:

**Human Error**: Mistakes in documentation or handling can lead to gaps in the chain of custody. Thorough training and clear procedures can help mitigate this risk.

**Technological Changes**: Rapid advancements in technology can make it challenging to keep up with proper evidence handling techniques. Investigators must remain informed about the latest tools and methods in digital forensics.

**Multiple Jurisdictions**: Cases that involve multiple jurisdictions may introduce additional complexities in maintaining the chain of custody. Collaborating with legal professionals familiar with local laws and regulations can help navigate these challenges.

## 5. Legal and Ethical Considerations

Maintaining the chain of custody is not only a best practice but also a legal requirement in many jurisdictions. Key considerations include:

**Compliance with Laws and Regulations**: Investigators should be familiar with relevant laws and regulations governing evidence handling in their jurisdiction. Compliance is essential for the admissibility of evidence in court.

**Ethical Handling of Evidence**: Investigators must act ethically when handling evidence, avoiding any actions that could compromise its integrity or lead to accusations of tampering or misconduct.

**Documentation of Consent**: When collecting evidence from individuals, particularly in private settings, obtaining proper consent is critical. Document the consent process to ensure compliance with privacy laws and regulations.

Maintaining a clear and well-documented chain of custody is vital for the integrity of digital evidence and the success of forensic investigations. By implementing best practices for documentation, secure storage, and personnel training, forensic investigators can ensure that the evidence remains credible and admissible in legal proceedings.

As technology continues to evolve, staying vigilant and proactive in maintaining the chain of custody will be essential for upholding the integrity of digital forensic investigations and ensuring justice in the digital age.

# Chapter 5: Analyzing Digital Evidence

In this chapter, we delve into the intricacies of analyzing digital evidence, a crucial step in the cybercrime investigation process. We will examine various analytical techniques, starting with file system analysis to uncover hidden or deleted data, followed by network traffic analysis to identify suspicious activity and communication patterns. Additionally, we will explore malware analysis, detailing how to dissect malicious software to understand its behavior and intent. By utilizing a combination of these methods, investigators can piece together a comprehensive picture of the cyber incident at hand. Throughout this chapter, we will emphasize practical approaches and real-world examples, empowering readers to develop the analytical skills needed to draw actionable insights from digital evidence and support effective decision-making in their investigations.

## 5.1 File System Analysis: Uncovering Hidden Data

File system analysis is a fundamental aspect of digital forensics, serving as a crucial method for uncovering hidden, deleted, or fragmented data within digital storage devices. By meticulously examining the file system structure, forensic investigators can recover valuable evidence that may have otherwise gone unnoticed. This chapter delves into the principles of file system analysis, the various file systems in use today, techniques for uncovering hidden data, and the challenges faced in this domain.

### 1. Understanding File Systems

A file system is a method and structure that an operating system uses to manage files on a storage medium. It determines how data is stored, organized, and retrieved. Different operating systems utilize various file systems, each with unique characteristics:

**FAT (File Allocation Table):** Used by older operating systems and some removable media, FAT is simple and widely compatible but lacks advanced features like journaling and permissions.

**NTFS (New Technology File System):** Common in Windows operating systems, NTFS supports advanced features such as file permissions, encryption, compression, and journaling, which help maintain data integrity.

**HFS+ (Hierarchical File System Plus):** Primarily used by macOS, HFS+ supports large files and is designed to handle complex metadata.

**ext4 (Fourth Extended File System):** Common in Linux environments, ext4 supports large volumes and files and features journaling for data integrity.

**APFS (Apple File System):** A modern file system for macOS and iOS, APFS is designed for flash storage and provides features like snapshots and cloning.

Understanding the structure and function of these file systems is essential for forensic analysts to interpret data correctly and recover hidden or deleted files.

## 2. The Importance of File System Analysis

File system analysis is crucial for several reasons:

**Recovery of Deleted Files:** When files are deleted, the file system often retains the data until it is overwritten. Analyzing the file system can reveal remnants of deleted files, allowing forensic investigators to recover potentially critical evidence.

**Uncovering Hidden Data:** Data may be intentionally hidden by users through techniques such as using hidden attributes or steganography. File system analysis can help identify and extract such data.

**Understanding User Behavior:** By examining file system metadata, investigators can reconstruct user activities, including file creation, modification, and access times, which can provide insight into the actions of individuals during the time of interest.

## 3. Techniques for File System Analysis

Several techniques can be employed in file system analysis to uncover hidden data:

**Examining File System Metadata:** Every file in a file system contains metadata that includes information such as file name, size, creation date, modification date, and last accessed date. By analyzing this metadata, forensic investigators can identify inconsistencies or anomalies that may indicate hidden or deleted files.

**Using File Carving:** File carving techniques can recover data by looking for known file signatures. Forensic tools can scan the unallocated space of a file system, identify remnants of deleted files, and reconstruct them based on their signatures, regardless of their current state in the file system.

**Analyzing Slack Space**: Slack space refers to the unused space in a storage cluster that is allocated to a file but not fully utilized. Investigators can examine this slack space for remnants of deleted files or hidden data that may not be visible through normal file system navigation.

**Investigating Alternate Data Streams (ADS):** In NTFS, files can contain alternate data streams that allow additional information to be stored alongside the primary file without altering its attributes. Forensic tools can reveal these streams, which may contain hidden or malicious data.

**Utilizing Journal Files**: For file systems that support journaling, such as NTFS and ext4, the journal files can provide a record of changes made to the file system. Analyzing these journal files can help reconstruct events and uncover data that might have been deleted or modified.

## 4. Challenges in File System Analysis

While file system analysis is powerful, it also presents several challenges:

**Encryption**: Many modern file systems employ encryption to protect data. If a file system is encrypted, accessing its contents without the proper keys can be impossible, limiting the effectiveness of forensic analysis.

**Fragmentation**: Files can be fragmented across the disk, meaning they are not stored in contiguous sectors. This fragmentation can complicate recovery efforts, as forensic investigators must piece together file fragments from various locations.

**Dynamic Data**: With the increasing use of cloud storage and dynamic file systems, data can change rapidly, making it challenging to capture a snapshot of the file system at a specific point in time.

**File System Corruption**: If a file system is corrupted, traditional analysis methods may fail. Forensic investigators may need to employ specialized recovery techniques to retrieve data from damaged file systems.

## 5. Tools for File System Analysis

A variety of tools are available to assist forensic investigators in file system analysis:

**Autopsy**: An open-source digital forensics platform that provides tools for analyzing file systems, recovering deleted files, and examining metadata.

**FTK Imager**: A forensic imaging tool that allows investigators to create images of storage devices and analyze file systems, including examining unallocated space and slack space.

**Sleuth Kit**: A collection of command-line tools for file system analysis that can perform tasks such as recovering deleted files and analyzing file system metadata.

**EnCase**: A comprehensive forensic tool that provides a wide range of capabilities, including file system analysis, data recovery, and reporting.

## 6. Legal Considerations

When conducting file system analysis, forensic investigators must adhere to legal and ethical standards:

**Authorization**: Ensure that proper authorization has been obtained before accessing and analyzing the file system. Unauthorized access can lead to legal repercussions.

**Documentation**: Maintain meticulous documentation of the analysis process, including the tools used, findings, and any actions taken. This documentation is critical for establishing the credibility of the evidence.

**Chain of Custody**: Follow established procedures for maintaining the chain of custody to ensure that the evidence remains intact and admissible in court.

File system analysis is a vital component of digital forensics, enabling investigators to uncover hidden, deleted, or fragmented data within storage devices. By employing various techniques and tools, forensic analysts can recover valuable evidence and gain insights into user behavior.

Despite the challenges inherent in file system analysis, adherence to best practices, legal considerations, and the use of advanced forensic tools can significantly enhance the effectiveness of investigations. As technology continues to evolve, staying informed about advancements in file systems and analysis techniques will be essential for successful digital forensic investigations.

## 5.2 Network Traffic Analysis: Monitoring Suspicious Activity

Network traffic analysis is a critical component of cybersecurity and digital forensics that involves monitoring, capturing, and analyzing data packets transmitted across a network. By examining network traffic, forensic investigators can identify suspicious activities, detect potential cyber threats, and gather valuable evidence for investigations. This chapter explores the principles of network traffic analysis, the tools used, the types of suspicious activities that can be identified, and best practices for effective analysis.

**1. Understanding Network Traffic**

Network traffic refers to the flow of data packets over a network, whether it be a local area network (LAN), wide area network (WAN), or the internet. Each packet contains essential information, including:

- **Source and Destination IP Addresses**: Identifying the origin and intended destination of the data packet.
- **Protocol Information**: Indicating which protocol is used (e.g., TCP, UDP, ICMP).
- **Port Numbers**: Specifying the communication endpoints for the source and destination services.
- **Payload**: The actual data being transmitted.

Analyzing this information is crucial for detecting anomalies that may indicate malicious activities, unauthorized access, or data breaches.

**2. Importance of Network Traffic Analysis**

Network traffic analysis is vital for several reasons:

**Early Detection of Threats**: By monitoring network traffic in real-time, organizations can detect suspicious activities early, allowing for rapid response to potential threats.

**Incident Response**: In the event of a cyber incident, network traffic analysis provides critical data that can help forensic investigators understand the nature and scope of the attack.

**Compliance and Auditing**: Many organizations are required to comply with regulations regarding data protection and cybersecurity. Regular network traffic analysis can help ensure compliance and provide documentation for audits.

**Understanding User Behavior**: Analyzing network traffic can help organizations understand how users interact with their systems, revealing patterns that may indicate inappropriate access or misuse of resources.

### 3. Techniques for Network Traffic Analysis

Effective network traffic analysis employs various techniques to uncover suspicious activity:

**Packet Capture**: This involves capturing data packets traveling over the network for detailed analysis. Tools like Wireshark and tcpdump are commonly used for this purpose, allowing investigators to inspect the contents of packets and identify potential anomalies.

**Flow Analysis**: Unlike packet capture, flow analysis focuses on the summary of network traffic over time. Tools like NetFlow Analyzer and sFlow allow analysts to visualize traffic patterns, making it easier to identify unusual spikes or drops in traffic that could indicate malicious behavior.

**Behavioral Analysis**: This technique involves establishing baselines for normal network behavior and monitoring for deviations from these patterns. Machine learning algorithms can be employed to detect anomalies automatically, flagging potential security incidents for further investigation.

**Protocol Analysis**: Analyzing the protocols used in network communication can reveal irregularities. For instance, if an unexpected protocol is detected on a particular port, it may suggest malicious activity or misconfigured services.

**Signature-based Detection**: This technique uses known signatures of malicious activity, such as patterns associated with specific malware or attack types, to identify threats. Intrusion Detection Systems (IDS) like Snort leverage signature-based detection to alert administrators of potential security breaches.

### 4. Types of Suspicious Activities Detected through Network Traffic Analysis

Network traffic analysis can help identify a variety of suspicious activities, including:

**Unauthorized Access Attempts**: Monitoring failed login attempts, unusual login times, or access from unfamiliar IP addresses can help identify potential intrusions or account compromises.

**Data Exfiltration**: Sudden spikes in outbound traffic may indicate that sensitive data is being transferred outside the organization, often associated with data breaches or insider threats.

**Malicious Software Communication**: Analyzing network traffic can reveal communication with known command-and-control (C2) servers, which is often indicative of compromised systems or malware infections.

**Denial of Service (DoS) Attacks**: Unusually high levels of traffic targeting a specific service or server can indicate a DoS or Distributed Denial of Service (DDoS) attack, where the goal is to overwhelm the system and render it unavailable.

**Network Scanning and Probing**: Repeated connection attempts to various ports or services can suggest that an attacker is scanning the network for vulnerabilities, indicating a potential reconnaissance phase of an attack.

**5. Tools for Network Traffic Analysis**

A variety of tools are available for network traffic analysis, each offering unique features for capturing and analyzing traffic:

**Wireshark**: A widely-used open-source packet analyzer that allows users to capture and interactively browse traffic in real time. Wireshark supports various protocols and provides extensive filtering options.

**tcpdump**: A command-line packet capture tool that is lightweight and useful for quickly capturing and analyzing traffic. It is especially valuable in environments where graphical interfaces are not available.

**NetFlow Analyzer**: A tool for monitoring traffic flows on the network, providing insights into bandwidth usage, traffic patterns, and potential anomalies.

**Snort**: An open-source intrusion detection and prevention system (IDPS) that analyzes network traffic in real-time and alerts administrators to potential threats.

**Suricata**: An advanced IDS/IPS capable of real-time intrusion detection and inline prevention, offering support for multiple protocols and advanced threat detection capabilities.

**6. Best Practices for Effective Network Traffic Analysis**

To maximize the effectiveness of network traffic analysis, forensic investigators should adhere to the following best practices:

**Define Baselines**: Establish normal traffic baselines for the network to facilitate the identification of anomalies and suspicious activities.

**Implement Continuous Monitoring**: Continuously monitor network traffic to detect suspicious activities in real time. Automated alerts can help identify threats promptly.

**Segment the Network**: Use network segmentation to isolate critical systems and limit access to sensitive data. This can reduce the attack surface and improve monitoring capabilities.

**Regularly Update Tools and Signatures**: Ensure that all analysis tools are kept up-to-date and that signature databases are regularly refreshed to include the latest threat intelligence.

**Conduct Regular Training**: Train staff responsible for network monitoring and analysis to recognize suspicious activities and respond appropriately.

## 7. Challenges in Network Traffic Analysis

Despite its importance, network traffic analysis faces several challenges:

**Volume of Data**: Networks can generate vast amounts of traffic, making it difficult to identify relevant events. Effective filtering and prioritization are essential.

**Encrypted Traffic**: Increasingly, network traffic is encrypted, which can hinder the ability to analyze its contents. Investigators may need to employ techniques to decrypt traffic when authorized.

**False Positives**: Automated tools may generate false positives, leading to alert fatigue and the potential for overlooking genuine threats. Continuous tuning and refinement of detection rules are necessary.

**Lack of Context**: Analyzing network traffic alone may not provide complete context for an incident. Correlating traffic analysis with other data sources, such as endpoint logs or user behavior, can provide a more comprehensive view.

## 8. Legal Considerations

When conducting network traffic analysis, forensic investigators must be aware of legal and ethical considerations:

**Authorization**: Obtain proper authorization before monitoring network traffic to ensure compliance with privacy laws and organizational policies.

**Data Retention Policies**: Adhere to data retention policies regarding how long network traffic data can be stored and under what conditions.

**Documentation**: Maintain thorough documentation of the analysis process, including findings, actions taken, and any communications related to the investigation.

Network traffic analysis is a vital practice in cybersecurity and digital forensics, providing insights into suspicious activities and potential threats. By employing various techniques and tools, forensic investigators can uncover valuable evidence and respond effectively to cyber incidents.

As technology continues to evolve and cyber threats become more sophisticated, staying informed about best practices and advancements in network traffic analysis will be essential for effective digital investigations. By implementing proactive monitoring strategies and adhering to legal and ethical standards, organizations can enhance their cybersecurity posture and improve their ability to detect and respond to threats in real-time.

## 5.3 Malware Analysis: Identifying Threats and Their Impact

Malware analysis is a crucial aspect of cybersecurity and digital forensics that focuses on understanding malicious software—commonly referred to as malware. This analysis aims to identify the characteristics, behaviors, and potential impacts of malware on systems and networks. By thoroughly analyzing malware, forensic investigators can develop effective countermeasures, enhance detection capabilities, and contribute to overall cybersecurity strategies. This chapter explores the types of malware, analysis techniques, the malware lifecycle, and the implications of malware threats.

### 1. Understanding Malware

Malware is a broad term that encompasses various types of malicious software designed to disrupt, damage, or gain unauthorized access to computer systems. Common types of malware include:

**Viruses**: Malicious code that attaches itself to legitimate files and spreads when the infected file is executed. Viruses can corrupt or delete data and cause system instability.

**Worms**: Standalone malware that replicates itself to spread across networks without needing to attach to a host file. Worms can quickly consume bandwidth and compromise multiple systems.

**Trojan Horses**: Malicious software disguised as legitimate applications or files. Users may unknowingly install Trojans, which can provide attackers with backdoor access to the system.

**Ransomware**: A type of malware that encrypts a victim's files and demands payment (usually in cryptocurrency) to restore access. Ransomware attacks have become increasingly common and impactful.

**Spyware**: Software that secretly monitors user activity and collects sensitive information, such as login credentials or personal data, often without the user's consent.

**Adware**: Software that automatically displays or downloads advertisements, often bundled with free software. While not always harmful, adware can compromise user privacy and system performance.

## 2. The Importance of Malware Analysis

Malware analysis is critical for several reasons:

**Threat Detection**: By analyzing malware, security professionals can develop signatures and heuristics to detect similar threats in the future, enhancing overall security measures.

**Incident Response**: Understanding the behavior and impact of malware is essential for responding to infections effectively. Analyzing malware allows investigators to determine the extent of the compromise and develop remediation strategies.

**Vulnerability Identification**: Malware analysis can reveal weaknesses in systems, applications, or user behaviors that can be exploited, helping organizations improve their security posture.

**Legal and Regulatory Compliance**: In many jurisdictions, organizations are required to take steps to prevent and respond to malware incidents. Thorough analysis can assist in meeting these obligations and demonstrating due diligence.

## 3. Malware Analysis Techniques

Malware analysis typically involves two primary approaches: static analysis and dynamic analysis. Each approach has its strengths and limitations.

**Static Analysis**: This technique involves examining the malware without executing it. Analysts look at the binary code, file structure, and any embedded resources. Static analysis helps identify known signatures, potential vulnerabilities, and obfuscation techniques. Tools commonly used for static analysis include:

**Disassemblers**: Tools like IDA Pro and Ghidra can convert binary code into assembly language, allowing analysts to study the program flow and identify functions and data.

**Hex Editors**: These tools, such as HxD, allow analysts to view and manipulate the binary representation of files, which can help uncover hidden strings and resources.

**PE (Portable Executable) Analyzers**: Tools like PE Explorer help analyze the structure of Windows executable files, revealing information about imported libraries, sections, and resources.

**Dynamic Analysis**: This technique involves executing the malware in a controlled environment, such as a sandbox or virtual machine, to observe its behavior in real-time. Dynamic analysis helps uncover how the malware interacts with the operating system, other processes, and the network. Key aspects of dynamic analysis include:

**Behavioral Analysis**: Monitoring system changes, file modifications, and network communications while the malware runs can provide insight into its functionality and objectives.

**API Monitoring**: Analyzing the API calls made by the malware helps identify how it interacts with the operating system and any attempts to manipulate system resources.

**Network Traffic Analysis**: Observing outbound network connections made by the malware can reveal command-and-control servers, data exfiltration attempts, or other malicious activities.

## 4. The Malware Lifecycle

Understanding the malware lifecycle is essential for effective analysis and response. The typical lifecycle of malware includes the following stages:

**Infection**: Malware is delivered to a target system through various vectors, such as phishing emails, malicious downloads, or compromised websites.

**Execution**: Once the malware is on the system, it executes its payload, which may involve establishing persistence mechanisms, escalating privileges, or performing reconnaissance.

**Communication**: The malware often communicates with a command-and-control server to receive instructions or exfiltrate data. Monitoring this stage is crucial for identifying the malware's objectives.

**Payload Activation**: The malware may activate its payload at specific times or under certain conditions, such as encrypting files in the case of ransomware or stealing credentials.

**Propagation**: Some malware types, such as worms, attempt to spread to other systems on the network, amplifying their impact.

**Persistence**: Malware may implement techniques to maintain its presence on the infected system, such as modifying startup programs or creating scheduled tasks.

**Data Exfiltration or Damage**: The final stage involves either stealing data, causing damage, or both, depending on the malware's objectives.

## 5. The Impact of Malware

The impact of malware can be significant and multifaceted:

**Financial Loss**: Organizations may incur substantial costs due to ransom payments, recovery efforts, system downtime, and loss of business. Ransomware, in particular, can lead to crippling financial losses.

**Data Breaches**: Malware can lead to unauthorized access to sensitive data, resulting in data breaches that compromise customer information and damage an organization's reputation.

**Operational Disruption**: Malware infections can disrupt business operations, leading to loss of productivity and delays in services.

**Legal and Regulatory Consequences**: Organizations that fail to protect against malware may face legal actions, fines, or sanctions, particularly if sensitive data is compromised.

## 6. Tools for Malware Analysis

A variety of tools are available for effective malware analysis, each serving specific functions:

**Cuckoo Sandbox**: An open-source automated malware analysis system that provides dynamic analysis capabilities, allowing analysts to observe malware behavior in a controlled environment.

**Malwarebytes**: An anti-malware tool that provides real-time protection and scanning capabilities, helping to identify and remove malware from infected systems.

**VirusTotal**: A web-based service that analyzes files and URLs for potential malware using multiple antivirus engines and provides insights into detected threats.

**Radare2**: A reverse engineering framework that supports various architectures and provides tools for binary analysis, including disassembly and debugging capabilities.

## 7. Challenges in Malware Analysis

Despite its importance, malware analysis presents several challenges:

**Evasion Techniques**: Malware developers often employ techniques to evade detection, such as obfuscation, encryption, and polymorphism, making analysis more difficult.

**Zero-Day Exploits**: New vulnerabilities that are unknown to the security community pose significant challenges for detection and analysis, as no signatures or behavioral patterns exist yet.

**Resource Intensive**: Dynamic analysis requires a controlled environment that simulates the target system, which can be resource-intensive and complex to set up.

**Rapid Evolution**: The malware landscape is constantly evolving, with new threats emerging frequently. Staying up-to-date with the latest threats and analysis techniques is essential for effective defense.

## 8. Legal Considerations

When conducting malware analysis, forensic investigators must consider legal and ethical issues:

**Authorization**: Ensure that proper authorization is obtained before analyzing potentially malicious files, especially when dealing with user systems or organizational data.

**Data Privacy**: Be mindful of privacy concerns and regulations, especially when analyzing malware that may interact with sensitive personal data.

**Documentation**: Maintain comprehensive documentation of the analysis process, findings, and any actions taken to ensure transparency and support legal proceedings if necessary.

Malware analysis is an essential component of modern cybersecurity and digital forensics, providing critical insights into the nature and impact of malicious software. By employing both static and dynamic analysis techniques, forensic investigators can identify threats, understand their behavior, and develop effective response strategies.

As the malware landscape continues to evolve, staying informed about emerging threats, analysis techniques, and best practices will be crucial for maintaining robust cybersecurity defenses. By investing in comprehensive malware analysis capabilities, organizations can enhance their ability to detect, respond to, and mitigate the impact of malware threats in an increasingly complex digital landscape.

# Chapter 6: Legal Considerations in Cyber Investigations

In this chapter, we navigate the complex legal landscape surrounding cyber investigations, highlighting the critical intersection of technology, law, and ethics. We will explore the various data privacy laws and regulations that govern the collection and handling of digital evidence, including the implications of the General Data Protection Regulation (GDPR) and the Computer Fraud and Abuse Act (CFAA). Additionally, we will discuss the challenges of ensuring the admissibility of digital evidence in court, including best practices for maintaining the integrity of evidence and adhering to legal protocols. Ethical considerations, such as the responsibilities of investigators to protect sensitive information and respect individual privacy, will also be addressed. By understanding these legal frameworks and ethical guidelines, readers will be better prepared to conduct thorough and lawful cyber investigations while upholding the rights of individuals and organizations.

## 6.1 Data Privacy Laws: Understanding Global Regulations

In today's digital age, data privacy has become a paramount concern for individuals, businesses, and governments alike. As the volume of personal data collected and processed continues to rise, so does the need for robust legal frameworks that protect individuals' privacy rights. Data privacy laws govern how personal information is collected, used, stored, and shared, providing a foundation for trust in the digital ecosystem. This chapter delves into key data privacy regulations from around the world, their implications for organizations, and the evolving landscape of data protection legislation.

### 1. The Importance of Data Privacy Laws

Data privacy laws are essential for several reasons:

**Protecting Personal Information**: These laws safeguard individuals' personal data from misuse, unauthorized access, and breaches, ensuring that people have control over their own information.

**Building Trust**: A clear regulatory framework enhances consumer trust in organizations that handle personal data. When individuals know their data is protected, they are more likely to engage with businesses.

**Mitigating Risks**: By adhering to data privacy laws, organizations can reduce the risks associated with data breaches, including financial penalties, reputational damage, and legal liabilities.

**Promoting Responsible Data Practices**: Data privacy regulations encourage organizations to adopt best practices in data handling, such as data minimization, purpose limitation, and transparency in data processing.

## 2. Key Global Data Privacy Regulations

Numerous countries have enacted data privacy laws to regulate the collection and use of personal information. Here are some of the most significant regulations:

**General Data Protection Regulation (GDPR) (European Union)**

**Overview**: Implemented in May 2018, GDPR is one of the most comprehensive data privacy regulations globally. It applies to all organizations that process personal data of individuals within the EU, regardless of where the organization is located.

**Key Provisions:**

- **Consent**: Organizations must obtain clear and explicit consent from individuals before processing their personal data.
- **Rights of Individuals**: GDPR grants individuals several rights, including the right to access, rectify, erase, and port their data.
- **Data Breach Notification**: Organizations must notify relevant authorities and affected individuals within 72 hours of a data breach.
- **Data Protection Officers (DPO):** Certain organizations must appoint a DPO to oversee compliance with data protection laws.

**California Consumer Privacy Act (CCPA) (United States)**

**Overview**: Enacted in January 2020, the CCPA is one of the most influential state-level data privacy laws in the U.S., focusing on the rights of California residents.

**Key Provisions:**

- **Consumer Rights**: California residents have the right to know what personal information is collected, the purpose of collection, and the right to opt-out of the sale of their data.
- **Data Access and Deletion**: Consumers can request access to their data and request deletion under certain circumstances.
- **Penalties for Non-Compliance**: Businesses can face fines for failing to comply with CCPA requirements.

## Personal Information Protection and Electronic Documents Act (PIPEDA) (Canada)

**Overview**: PIPEDA is Canada's federal privacy law governing how private-sector organizations collect, use, and disclose personal information in the course of commercial activities.

**Key Provisions:**

- **Consent**: Organizations must obtain individuals' consent when collecting personal information.
- **Access Rights**: Individuals have the right to access their personal information held by organizations and request corrections if needed.
- **Accountability**: Organizations are responsible for safeguarding personal information and must have policies and practices in place to comply with the law.

## Brazilian General Data Protection Law (LGPD)

**Overview**: Enacted in August 2020, the LGPD is Brazil's primary data protection law, closely mirroring the GDPR in its approach to data privacy.

**Key Provisions:**

- **Consent**: Explicit consent is required for data processing.
- **Data Subject Rights**: Similar to GDPR, individuals have rights concerning their personal data, including access, correction, and deletion.
- **Penalties**: Non-compliance can result in fines of up to 2% of a company's revenue in Brazil.

## Data Protection Act 2018 (United Kingdom)

**Overview**: The Data Protection Act 2018 supplements the GDPR and governs data protection in the UK, post-Brexit.

**Key Provisions:**

- **Compliance with GDPR**: Organizations must comply with GDPR as retained in UK law.
- **Special Categories of Data**: The Act provides additional protections for sensitive personal data.
- **Enforcement**: The Information Commissioner's Office (ICO) oversees compliance and enforcement.

### 3. Regional Considerations in Data Privacy Laws

Data privacy regulations vary significantly across regions, reflecting differing cultural, economic, and legal contexts:

**Asia-Pacific Region**: Countries in this region are increasingly adopting data protection laws. For example, the Personal Data Protection Act (PDPA) in Singapore sets out obligations for data controllers and rights for data subjects. In Japan, the Act on the Protection of Personal Information (APPI) governs data privacy and has been updated to align with international standards.

**Latin America**: Many countries are developing or updating their data protection laws. Mexico's Federal Law on Protection of Personal Data Held by Private Parties outlines data handling obligations, while Argentina has long been recognized for its strong privacy laws.

**Africa**: Data protection legislation is emerging across the continent. For instance, South Africa's Protection of Personal Information Act (POPIA) regulates the processing of personal information and aligns with global standards.

### 4. Compliance Challenges for Organizations

Organizations operating in a global context face several challenges in complying with diverse data privacy regulations:

**Complexity and Variability**: The differences in regulations across jurisdictions can create confusion and require organizations to adopt varied compliance strategies.

**Cross-Border Data Transfers**: Many regulations impose restrictions on transferring personal data outside of their jurisdiction. Organizations must navigate these rules, often requiring additional safeguards like Standard Contractual Clauses (SCCs).

**Resource Allocation**: Implementing compliance measures can be resource-intensive, necessitating investment in technology, staff training, and policy development.

**Evolving Regulations**: Data privacy laws are constantly evolving, requiring organizations to stay informed about changes and adapt their practices accordingly.

## 5. Future Trends in Data Privacy Laws

The landscape of data privacy laws is continually evolving, influenced by technological advancements, public awareness, and advocacy for stronger protections. Key trends include:

**Increased Regulation**: Governments around the world are likely to introduce or update data protection laws, driven by public demand for enhanced privacy rights and the need to address emerging threats.

**Stronger Enforcement**: Regulatory bodies are becoming more proactive in enforcing data privacy laws, resulting in higher penalties for non-compliance.

**Focus on Data Ethics**: There is a growing emphasis on ethical data practices, with organizations encouraged to adopt principles of transparency, fairness, and accountability in their data handling.

**Integration of AI and Automation**: As organizations increasingly rely on artificial intelligence and automated systems, data privacy regulations may evolve to address the complexities of algorithmic decision-making and data usage.

**Global Cooperation**: International efforts to harmonize data privacy laws may increase, with organizations advocating for consistency in regulations to simplify compliance across borders.

Data privacy laws play a vital role in protecting individuals' rights and fostering trust in the digital landscape. As the regulatory environment continues to evolve, organizations must stay informed about global data protection regulations and adopt comprehensive compliance strategies. By understanding and navigating the complexities of data privacy laws, organizations can safeguard personal information, mitigate risks, and build trust with their customers. The increasing importance of data privacy underscores the need for a proactive approach to compliance and responsible data management in an interconnected world.

## 6.2 Admissibility of Digital Evidence in Court

The rise of digital technology has transformed the landscape of legal proceedings, introducing new forms of evidence that can significantly impact the outcome of cases. Digital evidence—ranging from emails and text messages to documents and digital footprints—can provide critical insights into the facts of a case. However, the admissibility of this type of evidence in court is subject to specific legal standards and challenges. This chapter explores the criteria for the admissibility of digital evidence, the legal frameworks that govern it, and the best practices for ensuring that such evidence can withstand scrutiny in a courtroom setting.

**1. Understanding Digital Evidence**

Digital evidence is any information stored or transmitted in digital form that can be used to establish or refute facts in a legal investigation or proceeding. This includes:

**Documents**: Electronic files such as Word documents, PDFs, and spreadsheets that may contain relevant information.

**Communication Records**: Emails, text messages, and social media messages that can demonstrate intent, behavior, or interactions between parties.

**Metadata**: Data that provides information about other data, such as the creation date, modification history, and authorship of documents.

**Digital Footprints**: Data generated by users' interactions with online services, including browsing history, GPS location data, and account activity.

**Logs and System Records**: Information from computers and network devices that can indicate system access, user actions, and network activity.

**2. Legal Frameworks Governing Digital Evidence**

The admissibility of digital evidence is governed by several legal frameworks and principles, which may vary by jurisdiction. Some key concepts include:

**Federal Rules of Evidence (FRE):** In the United States, the FRE provides the foundational guidelines for the admissibility of evidence in federal courts. Relevant rules include:

- **Rule 401:** Defines relevant evidence as that which has any tendency to make a fact more or less probable.
- **Rule 403:** Allows the court to exclude relevant evidence if its probative value is substantially outweighed by the risk of unfair prejudice, confusion, or wasting time.
- **Rule 901:** Outlines the requirements for authentication of evidence, requiring that evidence must be shown to be what its proponent claims.

**Daubert Standard:** This standard is applied in federal courts and some state courts to evaluate the admissibility of expert testimony, including testimony related to digital evidence. The court must assess whether the expert's methods are reliable and relevant.

**Hearsay Rules:** Digital evidence may be subject to hearsay rules, which generally prohibit out-of-court statements from being admitted for the truth of the matter asserted. However, various exceptions may apply.

**Local Rules:** Courts may have specific rules regarding the submission and handling of digital evidence, including requirements for formatting, storage, and disclosure.

## 3. Criteria for Admissibility

To be admissible in court, digital evidence must typically meet the following criteria:

**Relevance:** The evidence must directly relate to the facts of the case and contribute to proving or disproving an element of the claim or defense.

**Authenticity:** The party presenting the evidence must demonstrate that it is genuine and has not been altered or tampered with. This often requires:

- **Chain of Custody:** A documented history of the evidence's handling, demonstrating that it has been preserved in its original state and has not been compromised.
- **Witness Testimony:** Testimony from individuals who can verify the authenticity of the evidence, such as IT professionals or law enforcement officers.

- **Reliability**: The methods used to obtain and analyze the digital evidence must be reliable and accepted within the relevant field. Courts often require expert testimony to establish the reliability of specific digital evidence.

**Compliance with Legal Standards**: The evidence must have been collected in accordance with applicable laws and regulations, including privacy laws and search and seizure laws.

## 4. Challenges in Admissibility

While digital evidence can be compelling, it often faces several challenges that may affect its admissibility:

**Alteration and Tampering**: Digital evidence can be easily altered, which raises concerns about its integrity. Courts may exclude evidence if there is a lack of confidence in its authenticity.

**Privacy Concerns**: The collection of digital evidence may involve privacy issues, particularly if data is obtained without a warrant or without the consent of the individuals involved.

**Complexity of Technology**: The technical nature of digital evidence can create challenges for judges and juries, who may not fully understand the nuances of digital forensics.

**Hearsay Issues**: Statements made in digital communications may be classified as hearsay, which can complicate their admissibility unless they fall under an exception.

**Expert Testimony Requirements**: The need for expert testimony to establish the reliability and relevance of digital evidence can lead to additional legal costs and complexity.

## 5. Best Practices for Admissibility

To enhance the chances of digital evidence being admitted in court, legal professionals and forensic experts should follow best practices:

**Proper Collection and Preservation**: Digital evidence should be collected using forensic methods that minimize the risk of alteration. This includes creating bit-by-bit copies of hard drives and ensuring proper documentation of the chain of custody.

**Documentation**: Maintain thorough records of the evidence collection process, including the time, date, individuals involved, and procedures followed. This documentation can help establish the authenticity and integrity of the evidence.

**Use of Expert Testimony**: Engage qualified experts to analyze digital evidence and testify about its relevance, authenticity, and the methods used in its collection and analysis.

**Stay Informed on Legal Standards**: Legal professionals must remain up-to-date on the evolving legal standards governing digital evidence, including relevant case law and regulatory changes.

**Prepare for Challenges**: Anticipate potential challenges to the admissibility of digital evidence and prepare counterarguments based on established legal principles and best practices.

The admissibility of digital evidence in court is a complex and evolving area of law that requires a careful understanding of legal standards and technical principles. As technology continues to advance and digital evidence becomes increasingly prevalent in legal proceedings, it is essential for legal professionals, forensic experts, and organizations to be aware of the requirements for admissibility. By adhering to best practices and staying informed about relevant legal frameworks, stakeholders can effectively navigate the challenges associated with digital evidence and contribute to the fair administration of justice. The role of digital evidence in legal proceedings underscores the importance of combining legal acumen with technical expertise in an increasingly digital world.

## 6.3 Ethical Considerations in Cyber Investigations

As cyber investigations become an integral part of law enforcement and corporate security measures, the ethical considerations surrounding them have gained prominence. The potential for misuse of digital tools, privacy violations, and the implications of digital surveillance necessitate a careful examination of ethical standards. This chapter explores the ethical dilemmas faced during cyber investigations, the importance of maintaining integrity and accountability, and the role of ethical frameworks in guiding investigators' actions.

**1. Understanding Ethical Principles in Cyber Investigations**

Ethics in cyber investigations pertains to the principles that guide the behavior of investigators in conducting their work. These principles often include:

**Integrity**: Investigators must conduct themselves honestly and transparently, ensuring that their actions are guided by a commitment to truth and justice.

**Respect for Privacy**: Cyber investigations often involve accessing sensitive personal information. Investigators must balance the need for information with individuals' rights to privacy, ensuring that data collection is both necessary and proportionate.

**Accountability**: Investigators should be held accountable for their actions, with mechanisms in place to review their conduct and decisions throughout the investigation process.

**Fairness**: Ethical investigations must be conducted impartially, without bias or discrimination. This includes treating all parties fairly and ensuring that investigations do not disproportionately target specific individuals or groups.

## 2. Common Ethical Dilemmas in Cyber Investigations

Cyber investigators frequently encounter ethical dilemmas that can complicate their work. Some of these include:

**Invasion of Privacy**: Investigators may need to access private communications, such as emails or messages, to gather evidence. This raises ethical questions about consent, privacy rights, and the extent to which personal information can be accessed without infringing on individual rights.

**Data Misuse**: The potential for data obtained during an investigation to be misused or mishandled is a significant concern. Investigators must ensure that data is used solely for its intended purpose and that safeguards are in place to prevent unauthorized access.

**Transparency vs. Confidentiality**: Investigators often operate in environments where transparency is critical for building trust, yet they may also need to maintain confidentiality to protect sensitive information. Balancing these two aspects can be challenging.

**Surveillance and Monitoring**: The use of surveillance technologies in cyber investigations raises ethical concerns regarding consent and the potential for overreach.

Investigators must be cautious about employing surveillance measures that may infringe on individuals' rights.

**Bias and Discrimination**: Cyber investigations can inadvertently perpetuate biases, especially when algorithms or automated systems are involved. Investigators must be vigilant in ensuring that their methods do not reinforce existing prejudices or discrimination.

## 3. The Role of Ethical Frameworks

Establishing a strong ethical framework is essential for guiding cyber investigations. Various organizations and professional bodies have developed codes of ethics and best practices that investigators can adhere to:

**Professional Codes of Conduct**: Organizations such as the International Association of Chiefs of Police (IACP) and the Association of Certified Fraud Examiners (ACFE) have established codes of ethics that outline the principles and standards expected of investigators.

**Guidelines for Ethical Cyber Investigations**: Specific guidelines can help investigators navigate ethical dilemmas. These may include recommendations for obtaining consent before accessing private data, ensuring that investigations are conducted with transparency, and establishing protocols for the responsible use of technology.

**Training and Education**: Providing ongoing training and education on ethical issues in cyber investigations is crucial. This can help investigators recognize ethical dilemmas, understand the implications of their actions, and develop strategies for addressing challenges in an ethical manner.

**Ethics Review Boards**: Some organizations have established ethics review boards to oversee cyber investigations, ensuring that ethical considerations are integrated into the decision-making process.

## 4. Legal vs. Ethical Considerations

It is important to distinguish between legal obligations and ethical considerations. While legal requirements set the minimum standards for acceptable behavior, ethical principles often demand higher standards. For example:

**Legal Compliance**: Investigators must comply with applicable laws, such as data protection regulations and privacy laws. However, ethical considerations may lead investigators to avoid practices that are technically legal but may be seen as exploitative or invasive.

**Informed Consent**: Legal frameworks may require investigators to obtain consent for data collection, but ethical considerations may call for additional transparency and communication to ensure individuals fully understand the implications of their consent.

**Proportionality**: Legal standards may permit broad data collection in certain circumstances, but ethical considerations advocate for a more measured approach that respects individual rights and minimizes intrusion.

## 5. The Importance of Ethical Cyber Investigations

Maintaining ethical standards in cyber investigations is crucial for several reasons:

**Public Trust**: Ethical practices foster public trust in law enforcement and investigative agencies. When individuals believe that their rights are respected and protected, they are more likely to cooperate with investigations.

**Legal Validity**: Ethical investigations are more likely to withstand legal scrutiny. Courts may be less inclined to admit evidence obtained through unethical practices, undermining the validity of the investigation.

**Organizational Reputation**: Organizations that prioritize ethical investigations enhance their reputation and credibility, reducing the risk of backlash from the public or regulatory bodies.

**Professional Responsibility**: Investigators have a professional responsibility to uphold ethical standards, which contributes to the overall integrity of the investigative process.

Ethical considerations in cyber investigations are essential for ensuring that justice is served while respecting individual rights. Investigators must navigate complex dilemmas that require a commitment to integrity, accountability, and fairness. By adhering to established ethical frameworks and continually educating themselves about ethical issues, cyber investigators can build trust, enhance the credibility of their work, and ensure that their investigations contribute positively to society. As the digital landscape evolves, so too must the ethical principles that guide those who navigate its complexities, ensuring that justice is achieved without compromising ethical standards.

# Chapter 7: Case Studies in Cybercrime Investigations

In this chapter, we delve into a selection of compelling case studies that illustrate the real-world application of cybercrime investigation techniques. Each case provides valuable insights into the challenges and successes encountered during the investigative process, showcasing a variety of cyber incidents—from data breaches and ransomware attacks to online fraud and harassment. By analyzing these examples, readers will gain a deeper understanding of the investigative strategies employed, the forensic methodologies utilized, and the lessons learned from both successful and failed investigations. This chapter not only highlights the practical aspects of cybercrime investigations but also emphasizes the importance of adaptability and critical thinking in addressing the dynamic nature of cyber threats. Through these narratives, readers will be inspired to apply the principles discussed throughout the book to their own investigative efforts.

## 7.1 Notable Cybercrime Cases: Lessons Learned

The landscape of cybercrime is vast and continually evolving, with numerous high-profile cases that have drawn public attention and shaped the development of cybersecurity measures and legal frameworks. These cases not only highlight the ingenuity of cybercriminals but also underscore the lessons that can be learned from each incident. This chapter explores several notable cybercrime cases, examining their backgrounds, the methods employed by perpetrators, the impact on victims, and the key takeaways that can inform future cybersecurity practices and investigations.

### 1. The Yahoo Data Breaches (2013-2014)

**Background**: In 2013 and 2014, Yahoo experienced two massive data breaches that exposed the personal information of over 3 billion user accounts. The breaches included sensitive data such as names, email addresses, phone numbers, and hashed passwords.

**Perpetrators**: Initially attributed to a state-sponsored actor, the breaches later involved criminal hackers seeking to sell the data on the dark web.

**Impact**: The breaches had far-reaching consequences, including a significant drop in Yahoo's valuation, legal repercussions, and a loss of user trust.

**Lessons Learned:**

- **Importance of Security Audits**: Regular security audits can help organizations identify vulnerabilities before they can be exploited.
- **User Awareness**: Companies should educate users about the importance of strong, unique passwords and two-factor authentication.
- **Incident Response Plans**: Organizations must have robust incident response plans in place to manage breaches effectively when they occur.

## 2. The Equifax Data Breach (2017)

**Background**: In 2017, Equifax, one of the largest credit reporting agencies in the U.S., suffered a data breach that compromised the personal information of approximately 147 million people, including Social Security numbers, birth dates, and addresses.

**Perpetrators**: The breach was attributed to vulnerabilities in the Apache Struts framework, which Equifax failed to patch in a timely manner.

**Impact**: The breach resulted in significant financial losses, including a $700 million settlement to affected consumers and regulatory fines. The incident also eroded consumer trust in Equifax and similar organizations.

**Lessons Learned:**

- **Timely Software Updates**: Organizations must prioritize timely patch management to protect against known vulnerabilities.
- **Transparency with Consumers**: Open communication about breaches and the steps being taken can help rebuild trust.
- **Data Minimization**: Organizations should collect only the data necessary for their operations to minimize exposure in the event of a breach.

## 3. The WannaCry Ransomware Attack (2017)

**Background**: The WannaCry ransomware attack in May 2017 affected over 200,000 computers in 150 countries, including hospitals, businesses, and government agencies. The ransomware exploited a vulnerability in Microsoft Windows and demanded ransom payments in Bitcoin.

**Perpetrators**: The attack was attributed to the North Korean hacker group known as Lazarus.

**Impact**: The attack caused widespread disruption, particularly in the UK's National Health Service, leading to canceled surgeries and delayed patient care.

**Lessons Learned:**

- **Regular Backups**: Organizations should maintain regular, secure backups of critical data to mitigate the impact of ransomware attacks.
- **Cyber Hygiene**: Basic security practices, such as using updated software and educating employees about phishing attacks, are vital in preventing malware infections.
- **Collaboration and Information Sharing**: Sharing information about threats and vulnerabilities among organizations can enhance collective cybersecurity defenses.

## 4. The Target Data Breach (2013)

**Background**: During the holiday shopping season of 2013, hackers infiltrated Target's payment system, stealing credit and debit card information from over 40 million customers. The breach was linked to a third-party vendor that provided Target with heating and air conditioning services.

**Perpetrators**: Cybercriminals used stolen credentials to access Target's network, demonstrating the risk posed by third-party vendors.

**Impact**: The breach led to significant financial losses for Target, including a $18.5 million settlement and damage to its reputation.

**Lessons Learned:**

- **Vendor Risk Management**: Companies must assess and manage the security practices of third-party vendors to protect sensitive information.
- **Advanced Threat Detection**: Implementing advanced threat detection systems can help identify and respond to suspicious activity in real-time.
- **Customer Communication**: Promptly informing customers about breaches and providing them with resources, such as credit monitoring, can help mitigate potential harm.

## 5. The Marriott Data Breach (2018)

**Background**: In 2018, Marriott International disclosed a data breach affecting approximately 500 million customers' personal information, including names, email addresses, phone numbers, passport numbers, and credit card information. The breach dated back to 2014, originating from the acquisition of Starwood Hotels.

**Perpetrators**: The breach was attributed to a sophisticated cyberattack by a group believed to be linked to Chinese intelligence.

**Impact**: The breach had serious implications for customer privacy and resulted in a lawsuit, regulatory scrutiny, and damage to Marriott's reputation.

**Lessons Learned:**

- **Due Diligence in Mergers and Acquisitions**: Organizations should conduct thorough cybersecurity assessments during mergers and acquisitions to identify and address potential vulnerabilities.
- **Long-term Monitoring**: Continuous monitoring of networks and systems is essential to detect and respond to breaches that may have occurred over extended periods.
- **Privacy Policy Transparency**: Clear and transparent privacy policies can help consumers understand how their data is being used and protected.

## 6. The Colonial Pipeline Ransomware Attack (2021)

**Background**: In May 2021, the Colonial Pipeline, a major fuel supplier in the U.S., was hit by a ransomware attack that forced the company to shut down its operations for several days. The attackers demanded a ransom of approximately $5 million.

**Perpetrators**: The attack was attributed to the DarkSide group, which exploited a weak point in Colonial's security protocols.

**Impact**: The shutdown led to fuel shortages along the East Coast and highlighted vulnerabilities in critical infrastructure.

**Lessons Learned:**

- Critical Infrastructure Protection: Organizations operating in critical sectors must prioritize cybersecurity to safeguard against potential attacks that can disrupt essential services.

- **Incident Response Readiness**: Developing and testing incident response plans can help organizations respond quickly and effectively to ransomware attacks.
- **Cyber Insurance Considerations**: Businesses should evaluate their cyber insurance policies and ensure adequate coverage for potential losses due to cyber incidents.

The notable cybercrime cases examined in this chapter underscore the complex and ever-evolving nature of cyber threats. Each incident provides valuable lessons that can help organizations improve their cybersecurity practices, enhance their incident response capabilities, and foster a culture of security awareness. As cybercriminals continue to adapt and innovate, it is essential for organizations to remain vigilant, proactive, and prepared to defend against emerging threats. By learning from past experiences and implementing robust security measures, organizations can better protect themselves and their stakeholders in an increasingly digital world.

## 7.2 Analyzing Investigation Strategies: Successes and Failures

Cybercrime investigations are complex, involving multiple layers of digital forensics, cross-border collaboration, and technical expertise. Each case, whether successful or fraught with challenges, provides critical insights into the effectiveness of investigation strategies. This chapter delves into key cybercrime investigations to examine successful strategies as well as pitfalls, offering valuable lessons to guide future efforts in fighting cybercrime.

### 1. Successful Investigation Strategies

Effective cybercrime investigations share certain core strategies that enhance their chances of success. Below are some exemplary tactics that have proven effective across major cases:

**Cross-Agency Collaboration**: Many successful investigations involve cooperation among various agencies and organizations, such as law enforcement, cybersecurity firms, and international bodies. For example, the takedown of the Silk Road marketplace was successful due to collaboration between the FBI, DEA, and other agencies, which combined resources and expertise across jurisdictions.

**Leveraging Threat Intelligence**: Cybercrime investigations benefit greatly from real-time threat intelligence. In the 2018 crackdown on the Andromeda Botnet, law enforcement utilized intelligence shared by cybersecurity firms to trace command-and-control servers, ultimately dismantling a network of infected devices worldwide. This shows how threat intelligence accelerates response times and reduces the risk of prolonged exposure.

**Advanced Forensic Techniques**: Sophisticated forensic methods, including network traffic analysis, malware analysis, and tracing cryptocurrency transactions, are essential in tracking down criminals. For instance, in the WannaCry ransomware investigation, researchers and law enforcement worked together to track Bitcoin transactions associated with ransom payments, narrowing down the source of the attack and attributing it to state-sponsored actors.

**Using Frameworks for Systematic Analysis**: Employing frameworks like the Cyber Kill Chain and MITRE ATT&CK helps investigators systematically analyze attacks, from reconnaissance to execution. This structured approach aids in identifying potential vulnerabilities and understanding the adversary's methods, enhancing the investigation's scope.

## 2. Pitfalls and Failures in Cybercrime Investigations

While many investigations succeed, others are hindered by specific obstacles. Recognizing these pitfalls can improve future investigative approaches:

**Lack of Jurisdictional Cooperation**: Cybercrime often spans multiple countries, and the lack of consistent cooperation can stymie investigations. For example, in the case of the Carbanak cyber gang, jurisdictional challenges slowed down law enforcement efforts because the group's operations and victims spanned over 40 countries. Without streamlined international collaboration, valuable time and leads were lost.

**Insufficient Cyber Resources**: Some investigations falter due to a lack of technical resources and expertise. Smaller law enforcement agencies may lack the budget and advanced tools required to handle complex cyber cases. For instance, early investigations into the Dark Web marketplace AlphaBay faced challenges due to limited resources, slowing down the initial efforts to trace its administrators and activities.

**Failure to Maintain Chain of Custody**: Adherence to chain-of-custody protocols is crucial for the admissibility of digital evidence. In some cases, mishandling evidence has led to legal challenges and even dismissal of cases. During a high-profile child exploitation case, for instance, improper data handling resulted in the inadmissibility of evidence, weakening the prosecution's case and underlining the importance of stringent handling protocols.

**Overreliance on Automation**: While automated tools and AI can speed up certain aspects of cyber investigations, overreliance can lead to false positives, overlooked evidence, or biased results. Automated tools sometimes flagged benign activity as malicious in the Fin7 cybercrime case, wasting resources and diverting focus from the actual perpetrators. A balanced approach, where automation supports rather than replaces human analysis, is often more effective.

### 3. Case Studies: Successes and Failures in Investigation Strategies

Several notable cases demonstrate both successful strategies and common pitfalls, offering a comprehensive view of real-world investigation dynamics.

**The Silk Road Investigation**: One of the most successful cyber investigations in recent history, the Silk Road case provides a blueprint for effective strategies. This case leveraged cross-agency collaboration, with the FBI, DEA, IRS, and other agencies pooling resources and intelligence. Advanced tracking methods, such as identifying patterns in IP addresses and tracing Bitcoin transactions, were crucial in locating the marketplace's founder, Ross Ulbricht. This case highlighted the importance of interagency cooperation, digital currency tracing, and forensic analysis.

**Operation Onymous**: In 2014, Europol coordinated Operation Onymous, an investigation that led to the shutdown of over 400 dark web sites involved in illegal activities. By sharing intelligence across 16 countries, investigators were able to systematically dismantle the infrastructure behind these sites. This case underscored the value of international cooperation and sharing forensic insights across borders to overcome jurisdictional challenges.

**The Target Data Breach Investigation**: The 2013 Target data breach revealed significant failures in cyber investigation strategy, mainly related to missed alerts and failure to act on early warning signs. Target's security system detected the malware activity, but due to a lack of protocol for handling such alerts, the investigation did not prevent or mitigate the breach in time. This case highlights the need for well-defined alert management processes and proactive threat response.

**The Colonial Pipeline Ransomware Response**: When Colonial Pipeline suffered a ransomware attack in 2021, its initial response faced scrutiny. The organization decided to pay the ransom to restore operations quickly, which led to public debate over the ethics of ransom payments and the risk of encouraging future attacks. However, the FBI's subsequent recovery of a portion of the ransom highlighted effective post-attack strategies, demonstrating the importance of collaboration between victims and law enforcement even after a ransom is paid.

**4. Key Takeaways for Effective Investigation Strategies**

From analyzing successes and failures in cybercrime investigations, several best practices emerge:

**Enhance Cross-Jurisdiction Collaboration**: Cybercrime knows no borders, making it essential to strengthen international partnerships and develop streamlined processes for intelligence sharing and cross-border enforcement.

**Invest in Specialized Training and Resources**: Continuous training for investigators on emerging cyber threats, new forensic tools, and global regulatory standards is essential. Dedicated resources for cybersecurity within law enforcement can empower teams to handle complex cases effectively.

**Develop a Proactive Incident Response Plan**: Having a clear incident response plan that includes alert protocols, communication plans, and digital forensic procedures enables quicker reaction times and minimizes damage.

**Balance Automation with Human Expertise**: Automated tools are invaluable for handling large datasets and detecting anomalies, but they should complement, not replace, human analysis. Analysts' insights are critical to interpreting data accurately, identifying subtle clues, and making nuanced decisions.

**Uphold Ethical Standards and Legal Protocols**: Adherence to ethical standards and chain-of-custody protocols protects the investigation's integrity and ensures evidence is admissible in court, preventing cases from being compromised.

Cybercrime investigations are high-stakes endeavors requiring a strategic combination of advanced tools, human expertise, and cooperation. The successes and failures in notable cases reveal that while technology plays a vital role, human factors—such as training, ethics, and interagency collaboration—are equally crucial. By learning from past cases and implementing refined strategies, organizations and law enforcement agencies can strengthen their approach to combating cybercrime, ultimately creating a safer digital landscape for all.

## 7.3 Interviewing Witnesses and Suspects: Best Practices

In cybercrime investigations, effective interviewing of witnesses and suspects is essential. These interviews can provide valuable insights into criminal methods, motivations, and networks. However, due to the technical and often complex nature of cybercrime, these interviews require specific techniques to yield reliable information and maintain the investigation's integrity. This chapter discusses best practices for interviewing witnesses and suspects in cybercrime cases, focusing on preparation, questioning techniques, and ethical considerations.

**1. Preparing for the Interview**

Preparation is the foundation of an effective interview. Investigators need to approach interviews strategically, informed by technical knowledge of the crime, the suspect's potential background, and relevant digital evidence.

**Researching the Case Background**: Before any interview, investigators should gather all available information, including digital logs, forensic evidence, and contextual details about the suspect's digital footprint and potential involvement. For example, if interviewing a suspect in a hacking case, the investigator might study relevant IP logs, communications, and activity on specific digital platforms to form precise questions.

**Understanding Cyber Terminology and Tools**: Cybercrime cases often involve jargon and specialized tools, such as VPNs, encryption software, or malware. Investigators must familiarize themselves with this terminology to engage meaningfully with suspects and witnesses, avoiding misunderstandings and demonstrating credibility.

**Developing a Question Strategy**: Crafting questions that progressively increase in specificity and complexity can help draw out more detail from interviewees. For instance, starting with open-ended questions allows suspects or witnesses to share general information before investigators ask more pointed questions to confirm or refute specific details.

**2. Questioning Techniques for Cybercrime Interviews**

Effective questioning strategies balance open-ended and closed-ended questions, helping investigators get a clear, truthful account while avoiding leading the interviewee toward specific responses. Techniques tailored for cybercrime cases can help in uncovering essential information.

**Establishing Rapport**: Building trust with the interviewee is crucial, especially in cases where the witness or suspect may be wary or uncooperative. Rapport-building techniques, such as showing understanding of the technical challenges they face or the complexities of digital environments, can help relax interviewees, making them more likely to share information.

**Using Open-Ended Questions**: Open-ended questions encourage interviewees to give detailed responses in their own words. For instance, instead of asking, "Did you access the company's database without authorization?" an open-ended alternative might be, "Can you describe your interaction with the company's systems?" This phrasing allows interviewees to explain their actions more naturally and often reveals additional information.

**Exploring Digital Evidence**: When presenting digital evidence, investigators should introduce it strategically, allowing interviewees to explain their understanding and interpretation of the evidence. For example, showing server log entries without immediate context might lead a suspect to explain the activity, inadvertently confirming or clarifying aspects of the investigation.

**Avoiding Technical Assumptions**: Cybercrime investigations frequently involve nuanced technical details that witnesses or suspects may misunderstand or misrepresent. By asking questions that clarify the interviewee's level of technical knowledge, investigators can better interpret their responses and avoid making assumptions about intent or capability.

## 3. Dealing with Challenges in Cybercrime Interviews

Cybercrime interviews are often more complex than traditional crime interviews due to factors like limited physical evidence, technical jargon, and the interviewee's possible denial of involvement based on digital anonymity.

**Handling Denial and Minimization**: Suspects in cybercrime cases may deny involvement, minimize their actions, or shift blame to technical factors. Effective interviewers respond by referencing specific digital evidence without revealing all available information. This method, known as strategic evidence presentation, encourages the suspect to provide a more accurate account without feeling entirely exposed.

**Navigating Digital Anonymity**: Cybercriminals often rely on anonymizing technologies like VPNs or the dark web. By asking questions that reveal the interviewee's understanding or use of these technologies, investigators can potentially link actions to the suspect's identity, even in cases where direct evidence is limited.

**Recognizing Deceptive Techniques**: Cybercrime suspects, particularly those with technical expertise, may use deceptive tactics or jargon to evade direct answers. Investigators can counteract this by staying informed on the latest cyber trends, which can help detect inconsistencies or deliberate misdirection in responses.

## 4. Ethical and Legal Considerations in Cybercrime Interviews

Ethics and legality are paramount when interviewing cybercrime witnesses and suspects, especially given the digital evidence involved and the potential for reputational damage. Respecting the rights of interviewees and maintaining integrity can protect the investigation from future legal challenges.

**Protecting Digital Privacy**: Witnesses and suspects in cybercrime investigations have rights concerning their digital privacy. Investigators should only use legally obtained digital evidence and respect boundaries around personal data, limiting questions to those directly relevant to the case.

**Ensuring Voluntary Participation**: While some interviews may involve individuals who are technically or legally savvy, it's essential to ensure that their participation in interviews is voluntary and informed. This is particularly relevant for interviews involving minors or employees with restricted access in corporate cybercrime cases.

**Avoiding Coercive Tactics**: Coercive techniques are not only unethical but may also render any obtained statements inadmissible in court. By adhering to non-coercive, fair interviewing techniques, investigators can gain insights without jeopardizing the integrity of the case.

## 5. Case Examples: Applying Best Practices in Cybercrime Interviews

Several notable cybercrime cases demonstrate the impact of effective interviewing techniques on the outcome of an investigation:

**The Case of Silk Road**: Investigators building the case against Ross Ulbricht, founder of the Silk Road darknet marketplace, used detailed digital evidence combined with patient interviewing strategies. By carefully presenting evidence of his online activities, investigators were able to link Ulbricht to his online pseudonym, "Dread Pirate Roberts," which played a pivotal role in his conviction.

**The Sony Pictures Hack (2014):** After the Sony Pictures hack, investigators faced challenges interviewing potential suspects and witnesses. By focusing on specific questions about knowledge of company networks, digital defenses, and communication patterns, investigators successfully narrowed down key individuals with insider knowledge, which helped in understanding the breach's scope and origin.

**Operation Onymous**: In the Europol-led takedown of numerous dark web sites, suspects interviewed were questioned about their knowledge and use of anonymizing tools like Tor. By exploring these suspects' technical understanding and reviewing their digital footprints, investigators gained insights into dark web activities that contributed to the operation's success.

Effective interviewing in cybercrime cases requires a nuanced understanding of digital evidence, careful preparation, and an ethically grounded approach. By combining open-ended questioning, rapport-building, and strategic evidence presentation, investigators can gain critical insights that move an investigation forward. The best practices discussed in this chapter, drawn from real-world successes and challenges, serve as a guideline for navigating the complexities of cybercrime interviews, ensuring that each conversation yields valuable information while upholding legal and ethical standards.

# Chapter 8: Social Media and Cybercrime

In this chapter, we examine the complex relationship between social media and cybercrime, exploring how these platforms can both facilitate criminal activity and serve as valuable sources of evidence for investigators. We will discuss various forms of cybercrime that thrive on social media, including identity theft, cyberbullying, scams, and misinformation campaigns. Additionally, we will highlight effective techniques for gathering and analyzing data from social media platforms, enabling investigators to track suspicious behavior, identify perpetrators, and connect with victims. As we navigate the ethical considerations surrounding the use of social media in investigations, this chapter will equip readers with practical strategies to leverage these platforms as critical tools in the fight against cybercrime, while also emphasizing the importance of respecting privacy and maintaining integrity throughout the investigative process.

## 8.1 Cyberbullying and Harassment: Evidence Collection

The rise of social media and online platforms has led to a new form of crime that exists almost entirely in digital spaces: cyberbullying and harassment. Collecting evidence in cases of online harassment presents unique challenges for investigators and victims alike, as these crimes often occur across various platforms, involve anonymous perpetrators, and can leave behind fragmented evidence. This chapter explores best practices for collecting digital evidence in cyberbullying and harassment cases, covering everything from the identification and preservation of relevant data to navigating platform policies and privacy considerations.

### 1. Identifying Evidence Sources

Cyberbullying and harassment typically involve multiple online interactions, making it essential to identify all potential sources of evidence. This can include not only obvious platforms, like social media and messaging apps, but also less apparent sources like email, comment sections, and public forums.

**Social Media Posts and Messages**: Cyberbullying often occurs in the form of direct messages, comments, and posts. Key platforms include Facebook, Instagram, Twitter, and TikTok, where perpetrators can engage in a mix of public and private messaging. For evidence purposes, it's crucial to gather screenshots, URLs, and timestamps of these interactions, ensuring that all relevant data is preserved.

**Chat Applications and Text Messages**: Harassment may extend into private messaging applications, such as WhatsApp, Telegram, and Discord. While some of these apps use end-to-end encryption, screenshots or exported chat histories can capture key exchanges, helping create a record of the harassment.

**Emails**: Some harassment, especially in professional settings, can occur over email. Documenting email exchanges, including sender information, timestamps, and full message content, is critical for a complete view of the behavior.

**Forum and Blog Comments**: Perpetrators may also leave harassing comments on forums, blogs, and public websites. These are often overlooked but can provide vital evidence, especially when paired with IP address data or usernames that connect to other platforms.

**2. Preserving Digital Evidence**

The transient nature of online communication makes it easy for harassers to delete or alter content, so preserving evidence quickly and effectively is paramount in these cases.

**Screenshots and Screen Recording**: The most direct method for preserving evidence is to take screenshots or use screen recording software to capture harassment in real time. When taking screenshots, ensure that timestamps, usernames, and platform information are visible to validate authenticity.

**Archiving Entire Webpages**: In cases where harassment occurs in comment sections or on social media pages, using web archiving tools can be helpful. Tools like the Wayback Machine or archive.today can capture a "snapshot" of a webpage, preserving it even if the original post is deleted.

**Metadata Collection**: Digital evidence often contains metadata, such as the date, time, and geolocation, which can be instrumental in building a timeline or linking activity to a particular user. While users can capture basic data with screenshots, tools like ExifTool or Forensic Toolkit (FTK) can extract additional metadata from images, messages, or files associated with harassment.

**Platform-Specific Download Options**: Some social media platforms allow users to download their entire history, which can be a valuable source of preserved evidence. Facebook, for example, lets users download all of their data, including messages, posts, and interactions, in a structured format that can serve as a comprehensive log.

## 3. Navigating Platform Policies and Legal Considerations

Different platforms have varying policies on data retention, privacy, and user data requests. Investigators must navigate these policies carefully to acquire evidence legally and ethically.

**Understanding Terms of Service and Data Retention Policies**: Each platform has its own rules for how long data is retained and what information is shared with law enforcement or investigative parties. Familiarizing oneself with these policies helps identify what data can be requested directly from the platform and what might be available only through legal channels.

**Using Subpoenas and Warrants**: For legally sanctioned investigations, subpoenas and warrants may be necessary to access private information from platform providers. In criminal cases, law enforcement may issue these to obtain IP addresses, login details, or other data that can link harassers to their activities.

**Privacy and Consent Considerations**: When gathering evidence of cyberbullying, it's essential to respect privacy laws, particularly in cases where minors are involved. In many regions, laws around digital privacy are strict, especially when minors are the target or the accused. Consent is often required from individuals to use data in legal proceedings, particularly in school or workplace settings where harassment is common.

## 4. Using Tools and Techniques for Enhanced Evidence Collection

Various digital forensics tools can streamline and enhance evidence collection in cyberbullying cases, ensuring that data is gathered systematically and effectively.

**Forensic Software**: Tools like FTK Imager, EnCase, and Cellebrite can assist investigators in gathering and analyzing digital evidence. These tools extract data from devices, gather metadata, and organize findings, making it easier to compile evidence in a manner consistent with legal standards.

**IP Tracking and Geolocation Tools**: In some cases, identifying the perpetrator's IP address and location can be essential for linking harassment to a specific individual. Forensic analysts often use network tools or work with ISPs to trace IP addresses associated with harassment, particularly for cases involving anonymous threats or stalking.

**Sentiment Analysis Software**: Advanced cases may benefit from sentiment analysis software, which helps investigators identify patterns in language or tone that characterize harassment. This type of analysis can substantiate claims of emotional harm, providing a quantitative perspective on the frequency and intensity of harassing language used by the perpetrator.

## 5. Best Practices for Reporting and Organizing Evidence

How evidence is documented and reported can significantly impact the outcome of a cyberbullying investigation. Clear, organized evidence not only supports the investigation but also provides a convincing case should the matter proceed to court or internal disciplinary action.

**Maintaining a Timeline**: Creating a detailed timeline of incidents can help investigators track patterns, establish intent, and highlight escalation over time. This timeline should include dates, times, platform details, and copies of the offending messages or content.

**Documenting Emotional and Psychological Impact**: Cyberbullying can have profound psychological effects on victims, often with legal relevance in harassment or stalking cases. Documenting any impact on the victim, including medical or psychological reports, journal entries, or witness statements, can support claims of emotional harm.

**Cross-Referencing Evidence**: In cases involving multiple platforms, cross-referencing evidence from different sources can provide a more comprehensive view. For example, if the perpetrator is using the same language or usernames across platforms, this can help substantiate their involvement and intent.

**Preparing for Legal Review**: Evidence should be organized in a format suitable for legal review, with clear labels, metadata, and an inventory. This ensures that digital evidence maintains its authenticity, admissibility, and credibility in legal settings.

Collecting evidence in cyberbullying and harassment cases requires a thorough understanding of digital platforms, technical tools, and legal considerations. By implementing best practices for identifying, preserving, and presenting evidence, investigators can more effectively combat online harassment, ultimately contributing to safer digital environments for everyone. Whether pursuing legal action or resolving the issue through other means, robust evidence collection lays the foundation for holding cyberbullies accountable and supporting victims in reclaiming their online spaces.

## 8.2 Fraud and Scams on Social Media Platforms

Social media platforms have become fertile ground for fraud and scams, with perpetrators exploiting the large user bases, trust networks, and relative anonymity to deceive victims. From financial scams and phishing schemes to identity theft and fake accounts, fraud on social media is growing increasingly sophisticated. This chapter dives into the various forms of fraud on social media, techniques for identifying fraudulent activity, and strategies for gathering evidence that can support investigation and prosecution.

**1. Common Types of Social Media Scams**

Understanding the different types of fraud that occur on social media platforms is essential to identifying and investigating these schemes. Scams often vary by platform, targeting specific user demographics and adapting to platform-specific features.

**Phishing and Impersonation Scams**: These scams involve attackers posing as trusted contacts, businesses, or support representatives to steal sensitive information. Common tactics include fake login pages, direct messages asking for personal details, and urgent calls for financial help. Scammers often use profile pictures and usernames that mimic legitimate accounts, making it challenging for users to distinguish real from fake.

**Investment and Cryptocurrency Scams**: A frequent and lucrative type of fraud, investment scams promise high returns in exchange for initial deposits. Scammers use fake testimonials, doctored images of bank statements, and posts showcasing supposed earnings. In cryptocurrency scams, perpetrators create fake accounts to promote "get-rich-quick" schemes, often enticing victims with fabricated success stories from well-known figures or influencers.

**Online Shopping and Giveaway Scams**: Fraudsters exploit users' interest in discounts and giveaways by setting up fake online stores, offering deals on popular products that never arrive. Giveaway scams are especially common, where fake accounts promise prizes if users "like," "share," or provide their information. These scams serve as data harvesting schemes, gathering contact information that can later be sold or used for other fraudulent activities.

**Romance Scams**: Romance scams typically target individuals seeking companionship. Perpetrators establish relationships with victims over weeks or months, eventually asking for money under false pretenses (such as medical emergencies or travel costs). These scams exploit users' emotional vulnerabilities, making them difficult to detect and prevent.

## 2. Identifying Fraudulent Activity on Social Media

Detecting fraudulent activity involves understanding the behaviors and red flags common to scammers. While social media companies have their own algorithms to detect and remove fake accounts, many scams go undetected, making it critical for investigators to recognize suspicious patterns.

**Analyzing Account Authenticity**: Genuine social media accounts usually have consistent activity histories, profile pictures, and connections. Fraudulent accounts, on the other hand, often exhibit signs of impersonation or fabrication, such as unusual usernames, limited followers, or recently created profiles. Reverse image searches can help verify profile photos to see if they've been used across multiple fake accounts.

**Monitoring Language and Interaction Patterns**: Scammers frequently use similar phrasing, vague messages, or scripted responses when communicating with potential victims. Investigators can look for signs of automated behavior or repeated phrases, especially in comments and direct messages. Unusual engagement patterns, like hundreds of likes or comments on a newly created account, are also indicative of fake or paid engagement.

**Tracking Suspicious Links and URLs**: Phishing scams often involve shortened or altered URLs that lead victims to fraudulent websites. By examining the structure and domain of a link, investigators can verify if a website is legitimate. Tools such as VirusTotal and Whois searches allow investigators to gather information about a link's origin and potential malicious intent.

**Identifying Patterns in Financial Activity**: In investment scams, money typically flows through anonymous payment methods, like cryptocurrency wallets, or digital payment apps that make tracing funds difficult. Investigators can gather data on these payment patterns, linking scammers across platforms or uncovering networks of related accounts engaged in similar activities.

## 3. Gathering and Preserving Evidence of Fraud

Collecting evidence of social media fraud is challenging due to the ephemeral nature of online interactions. Scammers often delete accounts, messages, and posts to erase their tracks, making early evidence collection vital.

**Capturing Screenshots and Metadata**: The first step in documenting fraud is to take screenshots of fraudulent profiles, messages, and any associated comments. Collecting metadata, such as the time and date of interactions, is also essential to establish a timeline. If feasible, investigators should capture the URLs of posts or accounts, as these may still be traceable even if deleted.

**Using Web Archiving Tools:** For persistent or widely circulated scams, web archiving tools can capture the scam's footprint across social media. Services like archive.today and the Wayback Machine allow investigators to save entire web pages, ensuring access to content that may be removed or altered.

**Tracking Financial Transactions and Cryptocurrency**: In cases involving financial loss, investigators can gather transaction records from victims. For cryptocurrency scams, blockchain explorers, such as Etherscan, allow for tracking of funds between wallets, potentially linking scams across cases. Payment providers and financial institutions can sometimes provide additional data about these transactions, though subpoenas may be required.

**Requesting Platform Data**: Social media companies hold valuable data that can be instrumental in fraud investigations, such as IP addresses, account creation details, and login histories. Investigators can request this information through official channels, although cooperation varies by platform and region. Subpoenas or court orders may be necessary for obtaining private user data.

### 4. Legal Considerations and Challenges in Social Media Fraud Cases

Social media fraud investigations intersect with various legal and jurisdictional challenges, given that platforms operate globally and perpetrators often reside in different countries than their victims.

**Jurisdictional Issues**: Fraudsters frequently operate across borders, complicating the investigation and prosecution processes. Collaborating with international agencies and understanding regional laws can help address these barriers, especially in high-stakes cases involving significant financial loss.

**Data Privacy Laws and Compliance**: Accessing personal data in fraud cases requires adherence to data privacy regulations like GDPR in the European Union. Investigators must carefully navigate these laws when requesting data from platforms, balancing the need for information with the individual's right to privacy.

**Admissibility of Social Media Evidence**: For evidence collected on social media to be admissible in court, it must be authentic and verifiable. Proper documentation practices—

such as noting timestamps, gathering supporting metadata, and ensuring a clear chain of custody—help build a robust case against fraudsters.

**5. Case Examples: Social Media Fraud in Action**

Real-world cases highlight the persistence and adaptability of social media scams and provide valuable lessons in investigative techniques.

**The Twitter Bitcoin Scam (2020):** In a high-profile hacking incident, attackers took control of several prominent Twitter accounts to promote a fake Bitcoin giveaway, promising to double any amount sent to a provided wallet. Investigators used blockchain tracking to monitor the flow of funds, ultimately uncovering the identities of the hackers and leading to successful prosecution.

**The Instagram Fake Product Scams**: Instagram has been a frequent platform for fake online stores, particularly in the fashion and electronics sectors. Investigators identified key red flags, such as cloned website designs and inconsistent branding, and worked with payment processors to halt transactions and protect future victims.

**The "Nigerian Prince" and Romance Scams on Facebook**: Romance scams, often linked to "Nigerian Prince" schemes, have proliferated on Facebook, with fraudsters targeting victims for money by fabricating emotional relationships. By analyzing transaction histories and linking IP addresses, investigators were able to dismantle several networks engaged in this form of social media fraud.

Social media fraud is an evolving challenge, blending social engineering with technological savvy to exploit unsuspecting users. By understanding common scams, detecting patterns of fraudulent behavior, and preserving evidence systematically, investigators can counteract these schemes effectively. The strategies outlined in this chapter provide a comprehensive approach to social media fraud investigations, equipping investigators with the knowledge and tools needed to combat scams, support victims, and uphold trust in digital spaces.

## 8.3 Using Social Media for Investigative Intelligence

Social media has become a critical tool for gathering investigative intelligence in both criminal and cybersecurity contexts. From tracking suspect behavior to analyzing networks of relationships, social media platforms offer investigators an invaluable wealth of information that can help solve crimes and build profiles of suspects. This chapter delves into how investigators can effectively use social media for intelligence gathering, discussing the types of information available, best practices for analysis, and the ethical and legal considerations involved in leveraging social media data for investigations.

### 1. Types of Intelligence Gathered from Social Media

Social media platforms host a diverse range of data that can be instrumental in investigations. This information can help analysts understand individual and group behaviors, uncover associations, and track activities in real time.

**Personal Information and Behavioral Patterns**: User profiles on social media often contain personal data such as location, employment history, interests, and daily routines. Investigators can leverage this information to map a suspect's movement, behavioral trends, and routines.

**Connections and Relationships**: Social networks reveal connections between people, showing who interacts with whom, how frequently, and in what contexts. Analyzing these relationships can help map out a suspect's network, revealing potential accomplices, associates, or even victims.

**Geolocation Data**: Many posts, especially those with photos or "check-ins," include geolocation tags that can pinpoint a person's exact location at specific times. By analyzing location data over time, investigators can build a timeline of a suspect's movements, potentially linking them to a crime scene or uncovering connections to other incidents.

**Visual Evidence**: Photos and videos shared on social media can reveal a range of useful information, from identifiable locations and clothing to associated vehicles and even weapons. Advanced analysis of visual evidence can uncover clues about activities, affiliations, or intentions that might not be immediately apparent from text alone.

### 2. Techniques for Social Media Intelligence Gathering

Successful social media intelligence gathering requires a combination of analytical skills, digital tools, and systematic approaches. By implementing the following techniques, investigators can maximize the effectiveness of their intelligence-gathering efforts.

**Keyword and Hashtag Analysis**: Tracking specific keywords and hashtags allows investigators to monitor relevant conversations and spot patterns. Social media listening tools like Hootsuite and Brandwatch enable real-time tracking of specific phrases, which can reveal popular topics, sentiments, and potential threats related to an investigation.

**Sentiment Analysis and Behavioral Profiling**: Sentiment analysis tools can help assess the tone of posts, comments, or discussions, shedding light on a suspect's intentions, attitudes, or emotional states. By profiling behavioral patterns, such as changes in language or tone over time, investigators may uncover indicators of escalating threats or identify underlying motives.

**Geofencing and Location Tracking**: Using geofencing tools, investigators can monitor posts and activities within a specific geographic area, which is particularly helpful for tracking events, identifying witnesses, or pinpointing suspect locations in high-crime areas. These tools help filter relevant posts by location, narrowing down the scope of investigation in areas of interest.

**Network Analysis**: Mapping connections on social media provides insights into a suspect's associations, uncovering relationships that are often hidden in plain sight. Network analysis tools like Maltego allow investigators to visualize social connections, revealing patterns of communication, clusters of connections, and even hidden ties to other suspects or criminal groups.

### 3. Ethical and Legal Considerations in Social Media Intelligence

While social media offers a wealth of information, using it for investigative intelligence requires a careful balance between legal compliance and ethical responsibility. Misuse of social media data can lead to privacy violations, legal repercussions, and public distrust, so understanding the ethical landscape is essential.

**Privacy Laws and Terms of Service**: Different jurisdictions have unique privacy laws governing the use of social media data for investigations. Additionally, each platform has its own terms of service that restrict how data can be accessed, stored, and used. Investigators must ensure they operate within legal guidelines and seek legal channels, such as warrants or subpoenas, where necessary.

**Consent and Public vs. Private Information**: Only public posts are typically accessible for intelligence purposes without a warrant; accessing private information without proper authorization can violate privacy rights. Investigators should focus on public data and respect the boundaries of private content unless formal legal permissions are granted.

**Data Storage and Handling**: Social media intelligence often involves the collection of large amounts of personal information, requiring careful handling to ensure security and compliance with data protection regulations. Establishing protocols for storing, accessing, and disposing of collected data can help protect both the investigation's integrity and individuals' privacy.

## 4. Tools and Platforms for Social Media Intelligence

Several tools are designed to assist investigators in collecting, organizing, and analyzing social media intelligence. By leveraging these resources, investigators can improve efficiency, accuracy, and depth in their analyses.

**OSINT (Open Source Intelligence) Tools**: Open-source intelligence tools like Maltego, SpiderFoot, and Social-Searcher are specifically designed to aggregate and analyze publicly available information. These tools enable investigators to monitor specific keywords, track public posts across platforms, and identify patterns that may be useful in building suspect profiles.

**Social Media Aggregators**: Aggregators like TweetDeck, Hootsuite, and Sprinklr allow investigators to follow multiple accounts, hashtags, and keywords across different social platforms in one place. These platforms streamline intelligence gathering by providing centralized access to real-time data from various sources.

**Sentiment and Language Analysis Software**: Sentiment analysis tools like Lexalytics or IBM Watson Natural Language Understanding help analyze the tone, intent, and mood of posts, which can be particularly helpful for threat assessment. Language analysis software can identify keywords, themes, and emotional cues, providing a deeper understanding of potential threats or intentions.

**Image Recognition and Metadata Extraction Tools**: Tools like Tineye and ExifTool enable investigators to analyze visual content shared on social media. Image recognition can help trace the origin of photos, and metadata extraction can reveal hidden data, such as geolocation or timestamps, aiding in the reconstruction of events.

## 5. Applications of Social Media Intelligence in Investigations

Social media intelligence can be applied across various investigative scenarios, from identifying threats to supporting criminal prosecutions.

**Tracking Suspects and Fugitive Locations**: Law enforcement agencies frequently use social media to track the whereabouts of suspects and fugitives. Publicly shared location data, check-ins, and live posts can reveal a suspect's recent activities and lead to their capture.

**Detecting and Preventing Threats**: Social media can act as an early warning system for detecting potential threats, especially for public events, high-profile individuals, or locations. By monitoring for threatening language, investigators can prevent incidents by intercepting suspects or warning potential victims.

**Building Case Evidence**: Social media evidence, such as messages, images, and timestamps, can substantiate claims and establish timelines, supporting court cases or internal investigations. Courts increasingly accept social media evidence as admissible, provided it's properly authenticated, making it an invaluable resource for building cases.

**6. Case Study: Social Media Intelligence in Action**

A real-world example of social media intelligence involves the investigation of the Capitol Hill riot in 2021. Law enforcement relied on social media posts, live videos, and shared photos to identify suspects and map out activities within the Capitol building. The open-source intelligence gathered from platforms like Facebook, Twitter, and Instagram allowed investigators to trace suspects' routes, identify connections among rioters, and build a detailed account of the events. This case underscored the value of social media intelligence, not only in real-time monitoring but also in post-incident analysis for accountability and prosecution.

Social media is an indispensable resource for gathering investigative intelligence, providing a real-time lens into behavior, relationships, and trends that are otherwise difficult to capture. By effectively utilizing open-source tools, understanding legal boundaries, and respecting privacy, investigators can gather actionable intelligence that aids in criminal investigations, threat assessment, and suspect profiling. As social media continues to evolve, so too will the opportunities and challenges it presents, underscoring the need for investigators to stay informed, adaptable, and vigilant in their approach to digital intelligence gathering.

# Chapter 9: Incident Response Planning

In this chapter, we focus on the essential elements of developing a robust incident response plan, which is vital for organizations to effectively mitigate the impact of cyber incidents. We will outline the key components of an effective incident response strategy, including preparation, detection, analysis, containment, eradication, and recovery. Emphasizing the importance of team roles and responsibilities, we will discuss how to assemble a skilled incident response team and establish clear communication protocols to ensure a coordinated response. Additionally, we will cover the significance of regular training and simulation exercises to keep the team prepared for real-world scenarios. By the end of this chapter, readers will have a comprehensive understanding of how to create and implement an incident response plan that not only minimizes damage during a cyber incident but also fosters resilience and learning for future challenges.

## 9.1 Developing an Incident Response Team

Building an effective Incident Response Team (IRT) is essential for any organization aiming to respond swiftly and efficiently to cyber threats. A well-prepared IRT can minimize the impact of security incidents, reduce downtime, and protect an organization's data and assets. This chapter explores the critical steps involved in developing an IRT, from defining roles and responsibilities to establishing communication channels and implementing response protocols. It also covers the skills and training necessary for a successful team and how to continuously improve the team's effectiveness through regular practice and post-incident analysis.

### 1. Defining the Roles and Responsibilities

Each member of an IRT has a specific role that is essential to an organized response to security incidents. Defining clear responsibilities ensures that team members understand their tasks and how they contribute to the overall response effort.

**Incident Response Manager**: The Incident Response Manager oversees the entire incident response process, coordinates team efforts, and makes strategic decisions. They're responsible for assessing the severity of incidents and ensuring proper actions are taken.

**Technical Specialists and Analysts**: These team members, often cybersecurity specialists, handle the technical aspects of incident investigation, containment, eradication, and recovery. Their roles may include malware analysis, forensic analysis, and vulnerability assessment.

**Communications Coordinator**: This role involves managing communication with internal stakeholders, affected parties, and external entities such as clients, partners, and media when appropriate. They ensure that accurate information is disseminated without compromising the integrity of the investigation.

**Legal and Compliance Advisors**: These advisors help ensure that all response actions comply with applicable laws, regulations, and industry standards. They assist in handling legal requirements for reporting incidents and guide the team on potential legal implications of the incident.

**Documentation and Reporting Specialist**: Documentation is vital to both tracking the incident as it unfolds and analyzing it afterward. The Documentation Specialist records all response activities, maintains logs, and produces a final report that can be used for audits, insurance claims, and future training.

## 2. Establishing Communication Channels

Efficient communication is essential for any incident response effort, especially in high-pressure situations. Establishing both internal and external communication channels helps ensure that information flows smoothly without delays or security risks.

**Internal Communication Tools**: The IRT should have access to secure, reliable communication tools that are separate from the regular network in case of a breach. Examples include dedicated email accounts, secure messaging apps, and emergency phone lines.

**External Communication Protocols**: Depending on the nature of the incident, the organization may need to inform external parties, such as customers, regulators, and law enforcement. Having predefined templates and a clear communication strategy can streamline this process and help maintain trust with stakeholders.

**Incident Severity Levels**: Establishing incident severity levels (e.g., low, medium, high, critical) helps prioritize response efforts and communicate the urgency to relevant parties. This tiered approach ensures that everyone, from the CEO to the technical staff, understands the gravity of the incident and their role in the response.

## 3. Developing an Incident Response Plan (IRP)

An Incident Response Plan (IRP) is the foundation of a successful IRT. This plan outlines step-by-step procedures for handling security incidents and serves as a roadmap for the team during a crisis.

**Preparation**: This phase involves setting up the team, acquiring necessary tools, and developing training programs to ensure readiness. It also includes setting up preventive measures like firewalls, intrusion detection systems, and regular software updates to reduce the likelihood of an incident.

**Identification**: The identification stage focuses on detecting and confirming security incidents. Effective identification involves monitoring systems, analyzing alerts, and gathering data to determine the scope and nature of the breach.

**Containment, Eradication, and Recovery**: Once an incident is identified, the team must contain it to prevent further damage, eradicate the threat by removing malware or closing vulnerabilities, and initiate recovery measures to restore affected systems.

**Post-Incident Analysis**: After resolving an incident, the IRT conducts a post-incident review to assess what went well and what could be improved. Lessons learned from these analyses can be used to refine response protocols and better prepare for future incidents.

## 4. Skill Development and Ongoing Training

A well-trained team is critical to the success of an IRT. Training should cover both technical and soft skills, ensuring that team members are prepared for a variety of incident scenarios and can work effectively under pressure.

**Technical Training**: Incident response requires expertise in various areas, including network security, malware analysis, forensics, and threat intelligence. Regular training sessions, certifications, and hands-on labs can help team members stay up-to-date with evolving cyber threats.

**Simulation Exercises**: Conducting regular simulation exercises, or "tabletop exercises," can help the IRT practice response procedures and prepare for real-life scenarios. These simulations reveal potential gaps in protocols and give the team a chance to practice working together under realistic conditions.

**Cross-Training and Collaboration**: Encouraging team members to cross-train in other roles within the IRT builds versatility and resilience. In case of an incident, cross-trained team members can step into different roles as needed, ensuring continuity and flexibility.

## 5. Maintaining and Evolving the IRT

A strong IRT is continuously evolving. Cyber threats and technologies change rapidly, so teams need to regularly update their skills, tools, and protocols to stay effective.

**Regularly Updating the IRP**: An effective IRP isn't static; it should be reviewed and updated frequently to reflect new threat intelligence, organizational changes, and lessons from previous incidents.

**Evaluating Tools and Technologies**: The tools used for incident detection, analysis, and response play a critical role in the team's effectiveness. The IRT should continuously evaluate its toolkit to ensure it includes the latest technology, such as endpoint detection and response (EDR) solutions, security information and event management (SIEM) systems, and other essential tools.

**Learning from Other Incidents**: A proactive IRT learns from other organizations' experiences as well. By studying high-profile incidents and analyzing what went well or poorly, the team can gain insights that might be applied in their own practices, enhancing their readiness and adaptability.

## 6. Real-World Example: Building a Strong Incident Response Team

To illustrate the importance of a well-organized IRT, consider the example of a large financial institution that experienced a major ransomware attack. The organization's IRT played a critical role in containing the attack, minimizing data loss, and restoring services in record time. Because the team had practiced their response plan, they quickly isolated infected systems, notified affected stakeholders, and coordinated with law enforcement. A post-incident review revealed that the team's strong internal communication and effective simulation exercises had been instrumental in their success, emphasizing the value of continuous training and structured response protocols.

Developing a capable, agile Incident Response Team is essential in today's digital landscape, where cyber threats continue to evolve in both sophistication and frequency. By clearly defining roles, maintaining effective communication, and providing continuous training, organizations can ensure that their IRT is equipped to handle security incidents with minimal disruption. Through diligent planning, regular practice, and a commitment to improvement, an IRT not only becomes a reactive force but a proactive asset in safeguarding the organization's security and reputation.

## 9.2 Creating an Incident Response Playbook

An Incident Response (IR) Playbook is a detailed guide that provides step-by-step procedures to follow during a cybersecurity incident. Unlike the broader Incident Response Plan, which outlines the overall approach, the IR Playbook offers tactical instructions for specific scenarios, such as ransomware attacks, phishing incidents, and insider threats. This chapter explores how to create an effective IR Playbook, outlining key sections, actionable steps, and best practices for creating a versatile, easy-to-follow resource that empowers teams to respond swiftly and accurately to cyber threats.

**1. Purpose and Importance of an Incident Response Playbook**

An IR Playbook is vital because it streamlines the response process, helping teams make swift, coordinated decisions during stressful situations. With a structured playbook, organizations can respond consistently and efficiently to incidents, minimizing damage and reducing recovery time.

**Guidance for Specific Threats**: Playbooks offer tailored responses for different types of incidents, addressing the unique characteristics and risks associated with each scenario, such as malware infections, Distributed Denial of Service (DDoS) attacks, or data breaches.

**Consistency Across Teams**: A playbook establishes a standard approach, ensuring that all teams follow the same protocol. This uniformity not only improves response efficiency but also aids in training new staff and maintaining compliance with regulatory standards.

**Empowering Rapid Response**: By providing detailed, actionable steps, the playbook empowers incident responders to act quickly and decisively, reducing the impact of the incident and ensuring a coordinated effort across teams.

**2. Key Components of an Incident Response Playbook**

An effective IR Playbook contains specific, repeatable steps and critical information for each type of incident. Here's an outline of essential components:

**Incident Types and Scenarios**: Clearly define and categorize incident types based on past experiences, risk assessments, and current threat landscapes. Typical categories include malware infections, phishing, insider threats, data breaches, and more. Each scenario should have a dedicated section in the playbook.

**Preparation Steps**: For each type of incident, outline preparatory measures that can help mitigate damage, such as enabling multi-factor authentication (MFA), updating firewalls, or securing sensitive data. Preparation also includes pre-configured tools, incident logging systems, and securing response communications.

**Detection and Identification**: Provide guidance on how to detect and verify each incident type. This includes using monitoring tools, analyzing alerts, assessing initial evidence, and determining the scope of the incident. Early identification helps prevent the spread of the threat and allows faster containment.

**Containment Procedures**: For each scenario, detail steps to contain the threat and prevent further damage. For example, in a ransomware attack, isolating infected devices and disconnecting them from the network are immediate containment actions.

**Eradication and Recovery Steps**: Outline the necessary steps to remove the threat and restore affected systems. This may involve patching vulnerabilities, restoring backups, or scanning for residual malware. Ensure that these steps include protocols for verifying that all traces of the threat have been eliminated before systems go back online.

**Post-Incident Review**: Once the incident is resolved, provide instructions for conducting a thorough post-incident analysis. This includes assessing response actions, gathering feedback from team members, identifying areas for improvement, and updating the playbook to reflect lessons learned.

## 3. Building Specific Playbooks for Different Incident Types

Each incident type has unique characteristics that require specialized response steps. Tailoring playbooks for each of these scenarios ensures that the response is thorough, targeted, and effective.

**Phishing Attacks**: The phishing playbook should include detection techniques, such as monitoring email filtering systems and identifying suspicious email content. Containment steps might include warning employees, quarantining emails, and assessing if any sensitive data was compromised. Eradication should focus on updating security protocols, and recovery steps may involve user awareness training.

**Ransomware Incidents**: Ransomware requires immediate containment measures, like isolating affected systems and disconnecting from the network. The playbook should include procedures for restoring data from backups and verifying that no malware remains before restoring systems. A detailed recovery protocol can help prevent recurrence.

**Insider Threats**: Addressing insider threats involves monitoring unusual access patterns, notifying legal and compliance teams, and conducting in-depth forensic analysis. Response actions in the playbook should include revoking credentials, securing sensitive data, and notifying affected parties if needed.

## 4. Establishing Communication Protocols

Clear communication is essential during incident response, as it ensures that team members are informed and aligned, and that external stakeholders receive accurate information without compromising the investigation.

**Internal Communication**: Define communication protocols for informing relevant teams, such as IT, legal, HR, and executive leadership, based on the severity and type of incident. Clearly outline who is responsible for initiating communication, what information to share, and how frequently updates are provided.

**External Communication**: Certain incidents may require communication with external stakeholders, such as clients, customers, regulatory bodies, or the media. The playbook should contain pre-approved messaging templates and guidelines for handling public disclosures to ensure compliance with legal requirements and maintain public trust.

## 5. Testing and Reviewing the Playbook

The IR Playbook is a living document that must evolve alongside new threats and technologies. Regular testing and reviewing are crucial to maintaining its effectiveness and ensuring that team members are familiar with response steps.

**Simulations and Drills**: Conducting regular incident response simulations and tabletop exercises allows the team to practice and become comfortable with the playbook steps. These exercises reveal gaps or potential points of confusion, allowing for timely updates.

**Post-Incident Reviews**: After every real or simulated incident, perform a post-incident review to evaluate what worked and what didn't. Use these insights to refine playbook entries, adding any new response tactics or deleting outdated steps as necessary.

**Continuous Updating**: Cyber threats evolve, and so should the playbook. Establish a schedule for regular reviews (e.g., quarterly or after significant changes in technology or regulations) to ensure that each playbook scenario remains relevant and effective.

**6. Case Study: A Ransomware Incident Playbook in Action**

Consider a healthcare organization hit by a ransomware attack, threatening patient data and disrupting essential services. With a ransomware-specific playbook in place, the response team followed these steps to contain the attack:

**Detection and Identification**: The playbook directed IT staff to verify unusual data encryption and lock-screen messages as indicators of ransomware. This quick identification allowed the team to start containment immediately.

**Containment**: The team disconnected affected systems, blocked external access, and notified staff to prevent further spread. Containment actions were critical in limiting the attack's reach and securing critical patient data.

**Eradication and Recovery**: Following the playbook's guidance, the team restored data from secure backups and scanned systems to ensure no residual malware remained. Thanks to the predefined procedures, the organization minimized downtime and resumed patient services rapidly.

**Post-Incident Review**: After recovery, a thorough review allowed the team to assess containment actions, communication, and backup efficiency. Updates were made to the playbook to improve response speed and incorporate lessons from the incident.

Creating an Incident Response Playbook is a proactive step that enhances an organization's ability to respond swiftly and effectively to diverse cyber threats. By outlining specific steps for each type of incident, defining clear communication protocols, and continuously testing and refining the playbook, organizations can empower their response teams to act with confidence and accuracy. In an era of growing cyber risk, a comprehensive, regularly updated IR Playbook is invaluable in protecting organizational assets, maintaining operational continuity, and securing sensitive data.

## 9.3 Post-Incident Review: Learning and Adapting

The Post-Incident Review (PIR) is one of the most critical stages in the incident response lifecycle. While the immediate focus in any cyber incident is containment, eradication, and recovery, the PIR helps organizations learn from each incident to strengthen their defenses and improve response efforts. This chapter delves into the importance of a structured PIR, covering best practices for conducting effective reviews, how to document findings, and how to integrate those lessons to prevent future incidents.

**1. Purpose of a Post-Incident Review**

A PIR provides an opportunity for organizations to understand what worked, what didn't, and how the response process can be improved. Its goal is to refine incident response processes, strengthen defenses, and build resilience against future cyber threats.

**Root Cause Analysis**: Identifying the root cause of an incident helps the organization address underlying vulnerabilities, whether technical, procedural, or human. By understanding how the incident occurred, the organization can prevent recurrence.

**Process Improvement**: By reviewing each step in the response, the PIR identifies gaps or inefficiencies. This can lead to revisions in the Incident Response Plan (IRP) and playbooks to ensure smoother and faster responses in the future.

**Building Organizational Knowledge**: PIRs also help build a knowledge base for the incident response team and the organization as a whole, adding practical insights that enrich future training and simulations.

**2. Steps in Conducting a Post-Incident Review**

A structured PIR process ensures that the review captures all essential aspects of the incident and response. The process includes gathering information, analyzing performance, documenting findings, and implementing improvements.

**Collecting Data**: Start by gathering all relevant data, including incident logs, alerts, emails, and notes from responders. Data collection should be comprehensive, capturing the timeline, actions taken, and decisions made during the incident.

**Incident Timeline and Key Events**: Constructing a detailed timeline helps clarify the sequence of events, highlighting points where response actions were effective and where they may have lagged. Key events include the initial detection, containment, eradication, and recovery phases.

**Evaluating Team Performance**: Review how well the incident response team performed in terms of communication, decision-making, and adherence to protocols. Evaluating each role provides insights into whether additional training or resources are needed.

**Communication Analysis**: Examine internal and external communication during the incident to ensure that information flowed smoothly to stakeholders, including team members, executives, and any affected clients or regulatory bodies.

**Assessing Technology and Tools**: Review the effectiveness of detection, containment, and recovery tools. If a particular tool or system fell short, it may need to be upgraded, reconfigured, or replaced.

## 3. Documenting Lessons Learned

Proper documentation is key to ensuring that lessons learned are accessible and actionable for future incidents. The PIR report should detail findings, insights, and recommended actions.

**Root Cause Identification**: Document the root cause(s) of the incident in detail, including technical, human, and process factors. This information is critical for understanding vulnerabilities and strengthening defenses.

**Successes and Failures**: Document what went well, such as quick containment or effective communication, as well as areas that need improvement. Being transparent about weaknesses helps build a culture of continuous improvement.

**Recommended Changes**: Include specific, actionable recommendations. This may involve updating playbooks, revising response procedures, or enhancing training programs to address identified gaps.

**Timeline Summary**: Summarize key events and timelines to give a clear overview of the incident flow. This is useful for future response team training and helps improve timing and efficiency in similar incidents.

## 4. Implementing and Tracking Improvements

Learning from an incident is only valuable if the organization takes steps to address the lessons learned. This involves integrating improvements into existing protocols, updating training, and ensuring that new measures are followed.

**Updating the Incident Response Plan (IRP):** Use the PIR findings to make targeted updates to the IRP, playbooks, and protocols. For example, if communication was delayed during containment, establish a streamlined communication protocol in the IRP.

**Adjusting Playbooks**: Playbooks for specific types of incidents should be revised to include new insights. If, for instance, a malware variant was challenging to eradicate, update the malware response playbook with new eradication strategies.

**Training and Awareness Programs**: Integrate PIR insights into training sessions to reinforce lessons learned. Consider conducting targeted training for the roles or areas that were found to be weak or unprepared during the incident.

**Tracking Progress**: Establish a tracking system for improvements. Assign ownership of each action item, monitor its progress, and conduct regular follow-ups to ensure changes are fully implemented.

## 5. Feedback Loop: Continuously Evolving the Incident Response Process

A successful incident response program relies on continuous improvement. Regular PIRs create a feedback loop that helps the organization stay ahead of evolving cyber threats.

**Routine Review and Testing**: Regularly revisit the IRP, playbooks, and procedures to ensure they reflect current best practices and threat landscapes. Periodic tabletop exercises and simulations can also test these updates in real-time.

**Incorporating Threat Intelligence**: Integrate new threat intelligence gathered during the incident into the organization's security measures and response procedures. This helps teams prepare for similar threats and strengthens preventative measures.

**Engaging Stakeholders**: Share PIR insights with key stakeholders, including senior management and external partners, to foster transparency and improve organizational buy-in for necessary changes.

## 6. Case Study: Applying Post-Incident Review for Continuous Improvement

Consider an organization that suffered a data breach due to a phishing attack. The PIR identified several critical insights:

**Root Cause**: A lack of employee awareness allowed the phishing email to bypass detection. Employees were unaware of how to spot phishing indicators, and the organization had not invested in a phishing-resistant email gateway.

**Response Gaps**: Initial detection was delayed due to ineffective monitoring, and communication among team members was inconsistent during the containment phase.

**Improvements Implemented**: The organization used these findings to implement a phishing awareness program, install an advanced email filtering solution, and update playbooks to ensure quick, coordinated action. They also streamlined communication channels, enhancing both efficiency and morale.

By addressing these gaps, the organization was able to build stronger defenses and a more agile response team, minimizing the likelihood of similar breaches in the future.

A Post-Incident Review is not merely a reflection on past events but a powerful tool for strengthening organizational resilience. By analyzing every aspect of an incident, from root causes to team dynamics, organizations gain invaluable insights that can guide improvements in policies, technology, and skills. Incorporating these lessons creates a robust feedback loop, continuously evolving the organization's readiness to respond to cyber threats. In an ever-changing digital landscape, the PIR process equips organizations with the knowledge and agility to adapt, respond, and recover faster with each incident, ultimately safeguarding their assets, reputation, and trust.

# Chapter 10: Emerging Technologies and Cyber Threats

In this chapter, we explore the dynamic intersection of emerging technologies and the evolving landscape of cyber threats. As innovations such as artificial intelligence, the Internet of Things (IoT), and blockchain gain traction, they introduce both new opportunities and vulnerabilities that cybercriminals are eager to exploit. We will analyze how AI can be weaponized for automated attacks and sophisticated phishing schemes, while IoT devices present unique security challenges due to their often limited defenses. Furthermore, we will investigate the implications of blockchain technology for cybersecurity, including its potential for secure transactions and the challenges posed by crypto-related crimes. By understanding these emerging technologies and their associated threats, readers will be better equipped to anticipate potential risks and develop proactive strategies to safeguard their digital environments against future cybercrime.

## 10.1 Artificial Intelligence: Benefits and Risks

Artificial Intelligence (AI) is reshaping the digital landscape, offering powerful tools for cybersecurity and cybercrime investigation while simultaneously introducing new risks and vulnerabilities. This chapter explores the dual role AI plays in today's cybersecurity arena: as a critical asset for detecting and responding to cyber threats, and as a potential weapon leveraged by cybercriminals to develop advanced, automated, and targeted attacks. Understanding both the benefits and risks of AI is essential for modern cybersecurity teams who aim to use this technology effectively while guarding against its misuse.

**1. Benefits of AI in Cybersecurity**

AI-driven tools bring significant advantages to cybersecurity, enabling faster response times, enhanced accuracy in threat detection, and advanced analytical capabilities. Below are some key benefits AI offers in the fight against cybercrime:

**Automated Threat Detection**: AI systems, particularly those powered by machine learning (ML), can analyze massive amounts of data to identify patterns and detect anomalies that may signal a cyber threat. These tools can flag unusual behavior or unauthorized access in real-time, helping cybersecurity teams respond more swiftly than they could through manual analysis.

**Enhanced Predictive Capabilities**: AI's predictive analytics can analyze trends and past attack patterns to anticipate future cyber threats. By identifying and assessing potential vulnerabilities, AI tools enable proactive security measures, reducing an organization's exposure to potential breaches.

**Improved Incident Response**: AI-driven systems can automate routine tasks during an incident response, such as scanning for compromised files, isolating affected systems, or patching vulnerabilities. This frees up human analysts to focus on more complex aspects of the investigation, improving overall efficiency and response times.

**Behavioral Analysis for Insider Threat Detection**: AI systems can analyze user behavior and detect signs of insider threats, such as unusual login patterns, access to sensitive information, or unauthorized downloads. This is particularly valuable in detecting malicious activity from trusted insiders, who may bypass traditional security measures.

**Continuous Learning and Adaptation**: Machine learning algorithms improve with exposure to new data, enabling AI tools to adapt to evolving cyber threats. As these systems learn from real-time incidents, they become more adept at identifying new or modified threats that might evade conventional detection methods.

## 2. Risks of AI in Cybersecurity

While AI offers substantial advantages, it also poses several significant risks. Cybercriminals are increasingly exploiting AI technologies for malicious purposes, and AI itself introduces new vulnerabilities and ethical concerns:

**Automated Attacks**: Just as AI can help defend against cyber threats, it can also enable cybercriminals to automate and enhance their attacks. AI-driven malware, for example, can autonomously adapt its behavior, evade detection, and spread more rapidly across networks than traditional malware.

**Deepfake Technology**: AI-powered deepfakes—highly realistic images, videos, or audio mimicking real individuals—pose serious security threats. Cybercriminals can use deepfakes to impersonate executives, commit fraud, or deceive individuals into disclosing sensitive information, a tactic known as "vishing" (voice phishing).

**AI-Generated Phishing**: Advanced AI algorithms can create highly convincing phishing emails tailored to individual targets. By analyzing public data or hacked information, AI can craft personalized messages that increase the chances of victims falling for phishing schemes.

**Data Poisoning Attacks**: Cybercriminals can deliberately introduce malicious or misleading data into AI systems, known as "data poisoning," corrupting the model and causing it to make incorrect decisions. For instance, by introducing poisoned data into an AI's training set, attackers could influence it to overlook specific types of malware or network intrusions.

**Bias and Ethical Concerns**: AI systems can inadvertently inherit biases present in their training data, leading to skewed or inaccurate threat assessments. Furthermore, the deployment of AI in cybersecurity raises ethical questions, such as the balance between enhanced surveillance and personal privacy, as AI can inadvertently collect, process, or misinterpret sensitive personal information.

### 3. Leveraging AI Responsibly in Cybersecurity

To harness AI effectively and ethically, cybersecurity teams must establish guidelines and safeguards that maximize AI's benefits while mitigating its risks. Responsible AI use in cybersecurity involves careful planning, oversight, and continuous evaluation of AI-driven tools and practices.

**Human-AI Collaboration**: Rather than relying solely on AI for decision-making, integrating AI tools with human expertise ensures balanced, informed responses to incidents. Human oversight helps prevent AI systems from misinterpreting data and supports ethical considerations in cybersecurity actions.

**Robust Testing and Validation**: Before deploying AI systems, rigorous testing and validation processes are essential. Cybersecurity teams should test AI-driven tools against a wide range of threats to evaluate their effectiveness and ensure that AI models do not overlook emerging attack patterns.

**Transparency and Accountability**: AI tools should be transparent, with clear documentation on how they operate and make decisions. Organizations should also assign accountability for AI-driven decisions, ensuring that ethical guidelines are followed, and unintended consequences are identified and addressed promptly.

**Safeguarding AI Models**: Protecting AI models from adversarial manipulation, such as data poisoning, is critical to preserving their integrity. Security teams must implement access controls, monitor data inputs, and periodically re-train AI models with verified, high-quality data to minimize vulnerabilities.

**Ethical AI Frameworks**: Developing an ethical framework for AI in cybersecurity can help organizations navigate challenges such as data privacy, surveillance, and bias. This includes following legal standards, like GDPR, for data handling and ensuring that AI use does not infringe on individual privacy rights.

**4. Case Study: AI in Action for Cyber Defense**

Consider an organization that implemented AI-driven anomaly detection software to enhance its network security. The AI system flagged unusual activity on a corporate server, detecting that an unauthorized user was accessing sensitive files during off-hours. Upon investigation, the cybersecurity team discovered a compromised user account, likely accessed via a brute-force attack.

**Real-Time Response**: The AI detected the unauthorized access within seconds, allowing the team to respond quickly, isolate the account, and prevent further access. This rapid response significantly minimized data exposure.

**Adaptive Learning**: As the system continued to monitor network activity, it adapted to the user behaviors and could later distinguish between legitimate access patterns and potential threats more accurately.

This case highlights AI's role in identifying sophisticated threats that may evade traditional detection methods. By enabling real-time, data-driven decisions, AI augmented the cybersecurity team's ability to safeguard sensitive information, underscoring the value of AI in fortifying network defenses.

**5. Preparing for the Future of AI-Driven Cybersecurity**

The use of AI in cybersecurity will continue to evolve, with both defensive and offensive AI tools becoming more sophisticated. As these technologies advance, organizations must stay vigilant, keeping pace with new developments and risks.

**Continuous Learning and Adaptation**: AI models require continuous updates to remain effective against evolving threats. Cybersecurity teams must implement processes to re-train models with new threat intelligence and adjust algorithms to detect emerging attack patterns.

**Investment in Skill Development**: Cybersecurity professionals must develop skills in AI and data science to manage AI-driven tools effectively. This knowledge empowers them to understand AI processes, address potential biases, and implement safeguards.

**Policy Development for AI Security**: Organizations should establish clear policies that outline acceptable uses for AI in cybersecurity, considering both legal regulations and ethical standards. Transparent, enforceable policies are essential for responsible AI adoption.

Artificial Intelligence represents both a powerful ally and a significant challenge in the realm of cybersecurity. When used responsibly, AI can automate threat detection, improve incident response, and help organizations proactively address vulnerabilities. However, AI also introduces risks, as cybercriminals exploit its capabilities to launch more sophisticated attacks. By understanding both the benefits and the potential pitfalls, cybersecurity teams can leverage AI strategically to protect assets and stay ahead of emerging threats. In an increasingly AI-driven future, balancing technological innovation with ethical and security considerations will be key to building resilient, adaptive cybersecurity defenses.

## 10.2 The Internet of Things: New Vulnerabilities

The Internet of Things (IoT) has transformed the digital landscape, connecting billions of devices worldwide, from smart home assistants and wearables to industrial machinery and critical infrastructure systems. While IoT devices enhance convenience, automation, and data-driven insights, they also introduce a vast and complex set of vulnerabilities that cybercriminals actively exploit. This chapter examines the unique security challenges of IoT, explores real-world vulnerabilities, and offers strategies to protect these devices in an increasingly interconnected world.

### 1. Understanding IoT Vulnerabilities

IoT devices operate with limited processing power and memory, making traditional security implementations difficult. Unlike traditional computers or servers, IoT devices are designed for specific functions with minimal cybersecurity features, making them susceptible to attacks. Here are some of the key vulnerabilities inherent to IoT systems:

**Weak Authentication and Authorization**: Many IoT devices have default passwords and lack multi-factor authentication options, making it easy for attackers to gain unauthorized access. Weak or absent authentication protocols increase the risk of brute-force attacks, especially on devices connected to sensitive networks.

**Lack of Regular Updates**: IoT devices often lack automatic update mechanisms, leading to outdated firmware with unresolved security flaws. Many device manufacturers don't prioritize updates, leaving vulnerabilities exposed long after they're discovered.

**Insufficient Encryption**: IoT devices typically communicate over wireless networks, often without strong encryption. This lack of secure communication protocols exposes them to interception, where attackers can capture or alter data in transit.

**Inadequate Physical Security**: Many IoT devices are deployed in remote or unsupervised locations, making them physically accessible to attackers. Physical access allows cybercriminals to tamper with devices, reset passwords, or directly extract data.

**Compatibility and Interoperability Issues**: The wide variety of IoT devices, operating systems, and communication protocols can lead to compatibility issues, resulting in security gaps. Additionally, interconnected systems increase the chances that a vulnerability in one device can affect others on the network.

## 2. Common IoT Attacks and Exploits

Cybercriminals exploit these vulnerabilities to carry out a variety of attacks, often with significant consequences for both individuals and organizations. Here are some common types of IoT attacks:

**Botnets**: A common IoT exploit involves taking control of vulnerable devices to form a botnet—a network of compromised devices under a single attacker's control. Botnets, like the notorious Mirai botnet, are often used in Distributed Denial of Service (DDoS) attacks, flooding servers with traffic to take down websites or services.

**Ransomware on IoT Devices**: IoT devices, especially in healthcare and manufacturing, have become targets for ransomware attacks. For instance, hackers might encrypt data on medical devices or machinery, demanding a ransom to restore functionality, which can severely disrupt operations.

**Data Exfiltration**: IoT devices collect vast amounts of data, from environmental conditions to user behaviors. If these devices are compromised, attackers can exfiltrate sensitive data, posing privacy and security risks. Data breaches from IoT devices can expose confidential information and create avenues for further attacks.

**Man-in-the-Middle (MITM) Attacks**: Without adequate encryption, IoT devices are susceptible to MITM attacks, where an attacker intercepts and manipulates communication between devices. For example, intercepted data from a home security camera could allow attackers to observe or tamper with video feeds.

**Physical Tampering and Device Hijacking**: IoT devices in insecure locations are at risk of physical tampering. Attackers can bypass the device's firmware, alter its function, or implant malware, turning it into a persistent entry point into the network.

## 3. Securing IoT Ecosystems

Given the unique constraints of IoT devices, securing these ecosystems requires a combination of robust design practices, network security measures, and ongoing management protocols. Here are some key strategies to mitigate IoT risks:

**Device Hardening and Configuration Management**: Proper device configuration is critical for IoT security. This includes changing default passwords, disabling unnecessary features, and enabling available security options. Device hardening should also involve regular checks and secure configurations tailored to each device's use case.

**Network Segmentation**: Isolating IoT devices on separate network segments helps limit access in case of a breach. For instance, placing IoT devices on a dedicated network separate from main IT infrastructure reduces the potential impact of a compromised device, preventing attackers from gaining access to other critical systems.

**Implementing Secure Communication Protocols**: Encryption protocols like Transport Layer Security (TLS) are essential to protect data transmitted between IoT devices and their controlling servers. Encrypted communication helps prevent MITM attacks, keeping data secure as it moves through various networks.

**Regular Firmware and Software Updates**: Ensuring that devices run on the latest firmware helps address known vulnerabilities. Manufacturers should prioritize automatic update mechanisms, and organizations using IoT devices must establish regular update schedules and policies for all devices within their network.

**Physical Security Measures**: For IoT devices deployed in public or unsupervised areas, physical security is vital. This can include tamper-proof cases, secure enclosures, and alarms that notify administrators if a device is accessed or tampered with.

**Monitoring and Incident Response**: Continuous monitoring of IoT device activity can help detect anomalies and potential threats early on. Implementing an incident response plan tailored to IoT devices allows organizations to quickly contain threats and recover from attacks targeting IoT infrastructure.

### 4. Case Study: IoT Vulnerabilities in Smart Cities

Consider a smart city project where IoT-enabled traffic lights, CCTV cameras, and environmental sensors are connected to a central monitoring hub. While this setup provides data-driven insights for urban planning and real-time traffic management, it also introduces a host of potential vulnerabilities.

**Challenges**: A lack of secure authentication on the traffic light system could allow attackers to alter light sequences, creating traffic congestion or even causing accidents. Insecure CCTV cameras could be accessed remotely, compromising citizens' privacy and law enforcement effectiveness.

**Mitigations**: To address these vulnerabilities, the city government implemented multi-factor authentication for critical systems and segmented networks so that any compromised device would not endanger others. Continuous monitoring of device activity and regular updates ensured that security threats were addressed promptly.

This case study demonstrates that while IoT technologies bring efficiency and intelligence to urban management, they require careful planning and proactive security measures to mitigate risks.

### 5. Future Directions in IoT Security

Securing IoT devices will continue to be a priority as the number of connected devices expands across industries. Here are some anticipated advancements in IoT security:

**Machine Learning for Threat Detection**: Integrating AI and machine learning into IoT systems can improve real-time threat detection by analyzing device behavior and identifying anomalies that indicate potential breaches.

**Blockchain for Secure Data Sharing**: Blockchain technology can create decentralized networks for IoT devices, securing data exchanges and reducing the risk of tampering or MITM attacks.

**IoT Security Standards and Regulations**: Industry and government initiatives are underway to establish IoT security standards and regulations. Compliance with such standards will encourage manufacturers to implement stronger security protocols and make updates a standard part of device lifecycle management.

The Internet of Things has revolutionized connectivity but has also introduced unique security vulnerabilities that organizations must address. By understanding the risks associated with IoT devices and implementing layered security measures—from robust device configuration to network segmentation and ongoing monitoring—organizations can better protect these systems and the sensitive data they handle. As IoT adoption continues to grow, proactive security practices and evolving technologies will be essential in minimizing the risks posed by an interconnected world.

## 10.3 Blockchain: Opportunities for Security and Investigation

Blockchain technology has gained significant attention in recent years, primarily due to its association with cryptocurrencies like Bitcoin. However, beyond its financial applications, blockchain offers transformative potential for enhancing security and facilitating investigations across various domains, including cybersecurity, data integrity, and digital forensics. This chapter explores the opportunities that blockchain presents for improving security measures, supporting cybercrime investigations, and addressing the challenges associated with emerging digital threats.

### 1. Understanding Blockchain Technology

At its core, blockchain is a decentralized, distributed ledger technology that records transactions across many computers in a way that the registered transactions cannot be altered retroactively without the alteration of all subsequent blocks and the consensus of the network. Key characteristics of blockchain include:

**Decentralization**: Unlike traditional databases maintained by a central authority, blockchain operates on a peer-to-peer network. This decentralization reduces the risk of single points of failure and makes it more difficult for attackers to manipulate the system.

**Transparency**: Each transaction on the blockchain is visible to all participants in the network. This transparency enhances accountability and enables stakeholders to verify transactions independently.

**Immutability**: Once a transaction is recorded on the blockchain, it becomes extremely difficult to change or delete it. This immutability is crucial for maintaining data integrity and preventing fraud.

**Consensus Mechanisms**: Blockchain networks rely on consensus mechanisms (e.g., Proof of Work, Proof of Stake) to validate transactions. These mechanisms ensure that all participants agree on the state of the ledger, further securing the network against malicious activities.

## 2. Opportunities for Security

Blockchain technology presents several promising opportunities to enhance security in various sectors:

**Data Integrity and Authentication**: Blockchain's immutable ledger can serve as a secure repository for sensitive data. Organizations can use blockchain to verify the integrity of data by storing cryptographic hashes of documents, transactions, or identity information. This ensures that any tampering is easily detectable.

**Secure Identity Management**: Blockchain can facilitate secure identity management solutions, reducing the risks of identity theft and fraud. Decentralized identity systems allow users to control their personal information, granting access only to authorized parties and minimizing exposure to data breaches.

**Supply Chain Security**: Blockchain enhances transparency and traceability within supply chains. By recording each step of a product's journey on the blockchain, organizations can verify the authenticity of products, prevent counterfeiting, and ensure compliance with regulations. This is particularly valuable in industries like pharmaceuticals, food safety, and luxury goods.

**Enhanced Cybersecurity Protocols**: The decentralized nature of blockchain can improve cybersecurity frameworks by distributing data across a network rather than storing it in centralized locations. This reduces vulnerabilities and the potential impact of attacks, such as ransomware, which typically target centralized databases.

**Smart Contracts for Automated Security**: Smart contracts—self-executing contracts with the terms directly written into code—can automate security protocols. For example, a smart contract can automatically execute a payment only when specific conditions are met, reducing the need for intermediaries and minimizing the risk of fraud.

### 3. Opportunities for Investigation

Blockchain technology also offers significant advantages for investigations, particularly in the realm of cybercrime and fraud:

**Forensic Analysis**: The transparent nature of blockchain allows investigators to trace the flow of transactions and identify malicious activities. By analyzing transaction patterns and timestamps, forensic analysts can uncover evidence of fraud, money laundering, or other illicit activities.

**Immutable Audit Trails**: Blockchain creates an unalterable record of all transactions, providing a reliable audit trail for investigators. This is particularly useful in cases involving disputes or allegations of misconduct, as the transparent record can serve as evidence in legal proceedings.

**Cross-Border Investigations**: The decentralized and global nature of blockchain facilitates international investigations. Law enforcement agencies can collaborate across jurisdictions, leveraging blockchain data to track criminal activities that span multiple countries.

**Cryptocurrency Tracking**: As cryptocurrencies become increasingly popular, tracking transactions on the blockchain can help investigators identify the flow of illicit funds. Blockchain analytics tools can analyze transaction data, allowing investigators to link wallets to real-world identities and trace the movement of funds across the network.

**Decentralized Data Sharing**: Blockchain enables secure and transparent data sharing among investigative agencies, law enforcement, and private entities. By utilizing blockchain, stakeholders can collaborate more effectively while maintaining data privacy and integrity.

### 4. Challenges and Limitations

Despite its promising benefits, the integration of blockchain technology into security and investigative practices faces several challenges:

**Scalability Issues**: Many blockchain networks struggle with scalability, leading to slower transaction processing times as the number of participants increases. This can hinder real-time applications, particularly in high-volume environments.

**Regulatory Uncertainty**: The legal status of blockchain technology and cryptocurrencies varies across jurisdictions. This lack of regulatory clarity can complicate investigations and hinder the adoption of blockchain solutions for security purposes.

**Complexity and Interoperability**: The diverse range of blockchain platforms and protocols can create interoperability issues. Organizations may face challenges integrating blockchain solutions into existing systems or collaborating across different blockchain networks.

**Data Privacy Concerns**: While blockchain offers transparency, it also raises concerns about data privacy. Public blockchains, in particular, expose transaction details that could compromise sensitive information. Balancing transparency with privacy is a critical challenge.

**Skills Gap**: The effective implementation of blockchain solutions requires a skilled workforce with expertise in blockchain technology and its applications. Organizations may struggle to find qualified personnel to manage and analyze blockchain data.

## 5. Future Directions for Blockchain in Security and Investigation

As blockchain technology matures, its potential for enhancing security and investigation will continue to expand. Here are some anticipated trends and developments:

**Regulatory Frameworks**: As governments and regulatory bodies establish clearer guidelines for blockchain technology, organizations will benefit from a more supportive environment for adopting blockchain solutions for security and investigation.

**Integration with AI and Machine Learning**: The combination of blockchain with AI and machine learning can enhance threat detection and investigative capabilities. AI algorithms can analyze vast amounts of blockchain data to identify patterns and anomalies indicative of fraudulent activities.

**Interoperability Solutions**: Efforts to develop interoperable blockchain platforms will facilitate collaboration and data sharing among various stakeholders, enabling a more comprehensive approach to security and investigations.

**Public-Private Partnerships**: Increased collaboration between public law enforcement agencies and private sector organizations will enhance investigative capabilities. These partnerships can leverage blockchain for data sharing, threat intelligence, and coordinated responses to cybercrime.

**Decentralized Autonomous Organizations (DAOs):** The rise of DAOs, which operate on blockchain protocols without central authority, presents opportunities for innovative approaches to governance and accountability in security and investigation practices.

Blockchain technology offers exciting opportunities for enhancing security and facilitating investigations in an increasingly digital world. Its decentralized, transparent, and immutable nature presents unique advantages in combating cybercrime, ensuring data integrity, and streamlining investigative processes. However, challenges such as scalability, regulatory uncertainty, and privacy concerns must be addressed to fully realize blockchain's potential. As organizations continue to explore the applications of blockchain, proactive efforts to integrate this technology into security frameworks and investigative practices will be essential for safeguarding against emerging threats and advancing the future of digital security.

# Chapter 11: Building a Cybercrime Investigation Team

In this chapter, we delve into the critical components of assembling an effective cybercrime investigation team, emphasizing the diverse skills and roles necessary for success in this complex field. We will discuss the essential qualifications and expertise needed for team members, including digital forensics, cybersecurity, legal knowledge, and analytical skills. The chapter will also highlight the importance of fostering a collaborative environment, where team members can leverage their unique strengths and share knowledge to tackle intricate cybercrime cases. Additionally, we will cover training and certification options that can enhance team capabilities and ensure members stay current with evolving technologies and threats. By the end of this chapter, readers will have a clear roadmap for recruiting, training, and managing a cohesive cybercrime investigation team that is well-prepared to confront the challenges of the digital landscape.

## 11.1 Essential Skills for Cyber Investigators

As cybercrime continues to evolve, the role of cyber investigators has become increasingly critical in identifying, mitigating, and prosecuting digital offenses. Cyber investigators operate at the intersection of technology and law, requiring a unique blend of technical skills, analytical thinking, and legal knowledge. This chapter outlines the essential skills that aspiring cyber investigators should develop to be effective in their roles and contribute meaningfully to cybersecurity efforts.

**1. Technical Proficiency**

Cyber investigators must possess a strong technical foundation, as their work often involves the analysis of complex digital systems and data. Key technical skills include:

**Digital Forensics**: Understanding the principles of digital forensics is crucial for examining devices and recovering data. Investigators should be familiar with forensic tools and techniques to extract evidence from various sources, such as computers, smartphones, and cloud services.

**Network Analysis**: Knowledge of networking concepts, protocols, and security measures is essential. Cyber investigators should be able to analyze network traffic, identify anomalies, and understand how data flows through different systems. This skill helps in tracing unauthorized access and uncovering malicious activities.

**Malware Analysis**: Investigators need to understand how malware operates and how it can compromise systems. Skills in reverse engineering and analyzing malicious software are crucial for identifying threats, determining their impact, and developing appropriate responses.

**Programming Skills**: Familiarity with programming languages, such as Python, Java, or C++, can greatly enhance an investigator's ability to automate tasks, analyze data, and understand how software operates. Programming skills can also assist in writing scripts for data extraction and analysis.

## 2. Analytical and Critical Thinking

Analytical thinking is paramount for cyber investigators, as they must assess vast amounts of data and identify patterns indicative of criminal behavior. Key components of analytical and critical thinking include:

**Data Analysis**: Cyber investigators must be proficient in analyzing large datasets to uncover trends and anomalies. Skills in data visualization and statistical analysis can help in presenting findings clearly and compellingly.

**Problem-Solving**: Investigators often face complex challenges requiring innovative solutions. The ability to approach problems methodically, identify potential solutions, and evaluate their effectiveness is crucial for successful investigations.

**Attention to Detail**: Cyber investigations often hinge on small details that can lead to significant breakthroughs. Investigators must possess meticulous attention to detail to ensure that no critical evidence is overlooked.

**Threat Intelligence Gathering**: Understanding the current threat landscape, including emerging trends and tactics used by cybercriminals, is essential for effective investigation. Cyber investigators should be skilled in gathering and analyzing threat intelligence from various sources.

## 3. Legal Knowledge and Compliance

A thorough understanding of legal frameworks and compliance requirements is essential for cyber investigators to ensure that their work adheres to laws and regulations. Key legal knowledge includes:

**Cybercrime Laws:** Familiarity with local, national, and international cybercrime laws is crucial for investigators to understand the legal implications of their work. This knowledge helps ensure that evidence is collected and handled in accordance with legal standards.

**Chain of Custody**: Cyber investigators must understand the concept of chain of custody, which involves maintaining the integrity of evidence from the moment it is collected until it is presented in court. Proper documentation and handling of evidence are critical to preventing challenges to its admissibility.

**Privacy Regulations**: Knowledge of privacy laws and regulations, such as the General Data Protection Regulation (GDPR) and the Health Insurance Portability and Accountability Act (HIPAA), is vital for ensuring that investigations respect individuals' rights and data protection principles.

**Compliance Standards**: Investigators should be aware of relevant compliance standards and best practices, such as those set forth by organizations like the National Institute of Standards and Technology (NIST) and the International Organization for Standardization (ISO). Adhering to these standards can enhance the credibility of investigations.

**4. Communication Skills**

Effective communication is a critical skill for cyber investigators, who must articulate complex technical concepts and findings to diverse audiences. Key communication skills include:

**Report Writing**: Investigators need to produce clear and concise reports detailing their findings, methodologies, and conclusions. Strong writing skills are essential for ensuring that reports are understandable to technical and non-technical audiences alike.

**Presentation Skills:** Cyber investigators often present their findings to stakeholders, law enforcement, or in court. The ability to present information clearly and persuasively, using visual aids when appropriate, is crucial for conveying the significance of their findings.

**Interpersonal Skills**: Cyber investigations often involve collaboration with law enforcement, legal teams, and other stakeholders. Strong interpersonal skills help investigators build relationships, share information, and work effectively within multidisciplinary teams.

**Interviewing Techniques**: Conducting interviews with witnesses, suspects, or victims is a common part of cyber investigations. Investigators should be trained in effective interviewing techniques, allowing them to gather information and assess the credibility of responses.

### 5. Continuous Learning and Adaptability

The rapidly changing nature of technology and cyber threats necessitates a commitment to continuous learning and adaptability. Key aspects include:

**Staying Informed**: Cyber investigators must keep up with the latest trends, technologies, and techniques in cybersecurity and cybercrime. Regularly reading industry publications, attending conferences, and participating in training sessions can enhance their knowledge and skills.

**Adaptability**: Cybercriminals are constantly developing new tactics, techniques, and procedures (TTPs). Investigators must be adaptable and willing to adjust their approaches in response to emerging threats and changing technology landscapes.

**Certifications and Training**: Pursuing professional certifications in cybersecurity and digital forensics, such as Certified Information Systems Security Professional (CISSP), Certified Information Security Manager (CISM), or Certified Cyber Forensics Professional (CCFP), can bolster an investigator's credentials and knowledge base.

The role of cyber investigators is increasingly vital in combating the rising tide of cybercrime. By developing essential skills in technical proficiency, analytical thinking, legal knowledge, communication, and adaptability, aspiring investigators can position themselves for success in this dynamic and challenging field. As cyber threats continue to evolve, the ability to investigate and mitigate these threats effectively will depend on a diverse skill set and a commitment to lifelong learning.

## 11.2 Training and Certifications in Digital Forensics

As the field of digital forensics continues to evolve in response to the increasing sophistication of cybercrime, the importance of proper training and certification for professionals in this domain cannot be overstated. Digital forensics investigators are tasked with uncovering, analyzing, and presenting evidence from digital devices and systems, which requires a deep understanding of technical concepts, legal frameworks, and investigative methodologies. This chapter explores various training programs and certifications available to those interested in pursuing a career in digital forensics, highlighting their significance and benefits.

**1. Importance of Training in Digital Forensics**

Training in digital forensics equips professionals with the knowledge and skills necessary to effectively handle and analyze digital evidence. The key reasons for pursuing training include:

**Technical Proficiency**: Training provides hands-on experience with various digital forensics tools and techniques, allowing investigators to become adept at evidence collection, preservation, and analysis.

**Legal Compliance**: Understanding legal standards and regulations is crucial in digital forensics. Training programs often cover topics related to the admissibility of evidence, chain of custody, and privacy laws, ensuring that investigators adhere to legal requirements.

**Best Practices**: Training emphasizes the importance of following established best practices in digital forensics, such as maintaining the integrity of evidence and conducting thorough investigations. Adhering to these practices is vital for ensuring the reliability of findings.

**Keeping Up with Technological Advances**: The digital landscape is constantly changing, with new technologies and threats emerging regularly. Training programs help professionals stay informed about the latest developments and equip them with the skills to address contemporary challenges.

**2. Popular Training Programs**

Numerous training programs are available for individuals pursuing a career in digital forensics. Some notable options include:

**University Degree Programs**: Many universities offer degrees in digital forensics, cybersecurity, or information technology with a focus on forensic investigation. These programs typically cover fundamental concepts, tools, and techniques in digital forensics while providing a broader understanding of computer science and cybersecurity principles.

**Boot Camps and Workshops**: Short-term intensive boot camps and workshops are designed to provide hands-on training in specific aspects of digital forensics. These programs often focus on practical skills, such as using forensic tools, conducting investigations, and analyzing digital evidence.

**Online Courses**: Online learning platforms offer a variety of courses in digital forensics, enabling individuals to learn at their own pace. These courses may cover topics such as mobile forensics, network forensics, and forensic analysis of various operating systems.

**Corporate Training Programs**: Many organizations offer in-house training programs for employees involved in digital forensics. These programs are tailored to the specific needs of the organization and may cover proprietary tools and processes.

## 3. Key Certifications in Digital Forensics

Certifications serve as a valuable way for professionals to validate their expertise and enhance their credibility in the field of digital forensics. Some of the most recognized certifications include:

**Certified Computer Forensics Examiner (CCFE):** Offered by the Information Assurance Certification Review Board (IACRB), the CCFE certification demonstrates proficiency in computer forensics principles and practices. Candidates are required to pass a comprehensive exam covering topics such as evidence collection, analysis, and reporting.

**Certified Forensic Computer Examiner (CFCE):** Administered by the International Association of Computer Investigative Specialists (IACIS), the CFCE certification focuses on practical skills in digital forensics. Candidates must complete a rigorous training program and pass both a written and practical exam.

**EnCase Certified Examiner (EnCE):** The EnCE certification is offered by Guidance Software and focuses on proficiency in using the EnCase forensic software suite. Candidates must pass a comprehensive exam that tests their knowledge of digital forensics concepts and their ability to utilize the software effectively.

**GIAC Certified Forensic Analyst (GCFA):** Offered by the Global Information Assurance Certification (GIAC), the GCFA certification focuses on the analysis of digital evidence and incident response. Candidates must demonstrate knowledge of digital forensics methodologies and pass a rigorous exam.

**Certified Information Systems Security Professional (CISSP):** While not exclusively a digital forensics certification, the CISSP credential, offered by (ISC)², is valuable for professionals involved in cybersecurity and digital forensics. It covers a wide range of topics, including security and risk management, asset security, and security operations, providing a well-rounded foundation for forensic investigators.

## 4. Benefits of Certification

Pursuing certification in digital forensics offers numerous benefits, including:

**Credibility**: Certifications signal to employers, clients, and peers that an individual possesses the knowledge and skills necessary to perform effectively in the field. This credibility can be particularly valuable when testifying as an expert witness in legal proceedings.

**Career Advancement**: Holding relevant certifications can enhance job prospects and open doors to advanced positions in digital forensics and cybersecurity. Many employers prioritize candidates with certifications when hiring for specialized roles.

**Networking Opportunities**: Certification programs often provide access to professional networks and communities, allowing individuals to connect with peers, share knowledge, and stay informed about industry trends.

**Continued Education**: Many certifications require ongoing education and recertification, ensuring that professionals remain current with the latest developments in digital forensics and cybersecurity.

## 5. Continuous Professional Development

In addition to formal training and certifications, continuous professional development is essential for digital forensics professionals. This can include:

**Attending Conferences and Seminars**: Industry conferences provide opportunities to learn from experts, attend workshops, and network with peers. Participating in these events helps professionals stay informed about emerging trends and best practices.

**Joining Professional Organizations**: Organizations such as the International Society of Forensic Computer Examiners (ISFCE) and the Association of Digital Forensics, Security, and Law (ADFSL) offer resources, training, and networking opportunities for digital forensics professionals.

**Engaging in Online Communities**: Online forums and communities focused on digital forensics provide platforms for knowledge sharing, problem-solving, and collaboration. Engaging with these communities can enhance professional development and support ongoing learning.

**Conducting Research**: Staying engaged in research and contributing to academic or industry publications can further establish expertise in digital forensics. This commitment to research helps professionals stay informed about the latest developments in the field.

Training and certification are critical components of a successful career in digital forensics. With the increasing complexity of cyber threats and the demand for skilled professionals, aspiring investigators must prioritize their education and ongoing development. By pursuing relevant training programs and certifications, individuals can equip themselves with the skills and knowledge necessary to navigate the challenges of digital forensics, contribute effectively to investigations, and advance their careers in this dynamic field. The commitment to continuous learning and professional growth will ensure that digital forensics investigators remain at the forefront of combating cybercrime and protecting digital assets.

## 11.3 Collaboration with Law Enforcement and Agencies

The fight against cybercrime requires a collaborative approach that brings together various stakeholders, including private sector professionals, law enforcement agencies, and governmental organizations. As cyber threats become more sophisticated and pervasive, effective collaboration is crucial for successfully investigating incidents, prosecuting offenders, and preventing future crimes. This chapter explores the significance of collaboration in digital forensics, the roles of different stakeholders, and best practices for fostering productive partnerships between cyber investigators and law enforcement agencies.

### 1. The Importance of Collaboration

Collaboration between cyber investigators and law enforcement agencies is essential for several reasons:

**Resource Sharing**: Law enforcement agencies often have access to resources, funding, and tools that may not be available to private sector investigators. By collaborating, both parties can leverage these resources to enhance their investigative capabilities.

**Expertise and Knowledge Exchange**: Cyber investigators and law enforcement personnel possess different areas of expertise. Collaborating allows for the sharing of knowledge about specific threats, vulnerabilities, and investigative techniques, ultimately improving the overall effectiveness of investigations.

**Faster Response Times**: In the face of rapidly evolving cyber threats, timely responses are critical. Collaboration enables investigators to quickly share information, alerts, and evidence with law enforcement, facilitating a more efficient response to incidents.

**Holistic Investigative Approach**: Cybercrime often transcends jurisdictions and involves multiple actors, including organized crime groups. Collaborating across different agencies and sectors allows for a more comprehensive understanding of the criminal landscape and the development of coordinated strategies to combat it.

## 2. Key Stakeholders in Collaboration

Several key stakeholders play essential roles in collaboration efforts to combat cybercrime:

**Cyber Investigators**: Professionals in private organizations, consulting firms, or academia who conduct digital forensics investigations. They often possess specialized technical skills and knowledge of cybersecurity practices that are valuable to law enforcement.

**Law Enforcement Agencies**: Local, state, and federal law enforcement organizations responsible for investigating and prosecuting cybercrime. These agencies have the legal authority to gather evidence, execute search warrants, and pursue criminal charges.

**Government Agencies**: National cybersecurity agencies, such as the Federal Bureau of Investigation (FBI) in the United States or the European Union Agency for Cybersecurity (ENISA) in Europe, play critical roles in setting policies, providing resources, and facilitating collaboration among various stakeholders.

**Industry Partners**: Technology companies, cybersecurity firms, and other private sector organizations contribute valuable resources, intelligence, and expertise. Collaborating with industry partners can help law enforcement stay informed about emerging threats and access cutting-edge technologies.

**International Organizations**: Given the global nature of cybercrime, international collaboration is essential. Organizations such as INTERPOL and Europol facilitate cooperation between law enforcement agencies across borders, enabling them to address cybercrime more effectively.

### 3. Best Practices for Collaboration

To foster effective collaboration between cyber investigators and law enforcement agencies, several best practices should be followed:

**Establish Clear Communication Channels**: Open lines of communication are critical for successful collaboration. Regular meetings, secure communication platforms, and dedicated liaison officers can help ensure that information flows smoothly between parties.

**Define Roles and Responsibilities**: Clearly defining the roles and responsibilities of each stakeholder involved in the investigation helps avoid confusion and ensures that all parties understand their contributions to the collaborative effort.

**Create Joint Task Forces**: Forming joint task forces composed of representatives from both cyber investigation teams and law enforcement agencies can facilitate coordinated responses to cyber incidents. These task forces can share resources, intelligence, and expertise to enhance investigative efforts.

**Implement Training Programs**: Providing joint training programs for cyber investigators and law enforcement personnel can improve understanding and cooperation. Training sessions focused on digital forensics techniques, legal considerations, and investigative methodologies can bridge the gap between sectors.

**Develop Standard Operating Procedures (SOPs):** Establishing SOPs for collaboration can streamline processes and ensure that investigations are conducted consistently. SOPs should cover aspects such as evidence collection, reporting, and communication protocols.

**Leverage Technology for Collaboration**: Utilizing secure technology platforms for information sharing and collaboration can enhance the efficiency and effectiveness of joint investigations. Collaborative tools, such as case management systems and secure file-sharing platforms, can facilitate information exchange while protecting sensitive data.

## 4. Challenges in Collaboration

While collaboration is crucial, several challenges can hinder effective partnerships between cyber investigators and law enforcement agencies:

**Jurisdictional Issues**: Cybercrime often transcends geographic boundaries, making it difficult to navigate jurisdictional challenges. Investigators must understand the legal frameworks governing their operations in different regions, which can complicate collaboration efforts.

**Resource Constraints**: Both cyber investigation teams and law enforcement agencies may face resource constraints that limit their ability to collaborate effectively. Budget limitations, personnel shortages, and competing priorities can pose challenges to successful partnerships.

**Cultural Differences**: Differences in organizational culture, practices, and priorities can create misunderstandings between cyber investigators and law enforcement personnel. Fostering mutual respect and understanding is crucial for overcoming these cultural barriers.

**Data Privacy Concerns**: Collaboration often involves sharing sensitive data and personal information. Investigators must navigate privacy regulations and ethical considerations to ensure compliance while still effectively sharing necessary information.

## 5. Case Studies of Successful Collaboration

Examining successful case studies of collaboration between cyber investigators and law enforcement can provide valuable insights and inspiration for future partnerships:

**Operation AILF**: This operation involved collaboration between private cybersecurity firms and law enforcement agencies to dismantle a major cybercrime syndicate involved in credit card fraud. By sharing intelligence and resources, the joint task force was able to trace the syndicate's operations, leading to multiple arrests and significant financial recovery for victims.

**The FBI's Cyber Action Team**: The FBI established the Cyber Action Team to provide rapid response capabilities for cyber incidents. This team collaborates with private sector partners to address high-profile cybercrime cases, ensuring that investigations are conducted efficiently and effectively.

**International Collaborations**: Joint operations conducted by INTERPOL and Europol have successfully targeted transnational cybercrime groups. By pooling resources and expertise from various countries, these organizations have been able to disrupt complex criminal networks that operate across borders.

Collaboration between cyber investigators and law enforcement agencies is essential for combating the growing threat of cybercrime. By establishing clear communication channels, defining roles, and implementing best practices, stakeholders can work together more effectively to investigate and prosecute cyber offenses. While challenges may arise, successful collaborations can lead to improved outcomes, greater resource efficiency, and enhanced knowledge sharing. As cybercrime continues to evolve, the importance of collaboration in digital forensics will only grow, necessitating ongoing efforts to strengthen partnerships and foster a united front against cyber threats.

# Chapter 12: Future Trends in Cybercrime and Investigation

In this chapter, we look ahead to the future of cybercrime and the evolving strategies needed for effective investigation in an increasingly complex digital landscape. We will explore anticipated trends, such as the rise of sophisticated ransomware attacks, the implications of quantum computing on encryption, and the challenges posed by deepfakes and misinformation. Additionally, we will discuss how advancements in artificial intelligence may reshape both criminal tactics and investigative methods, highlighting the need for adaptive strategies in response to these changes. By examining these emerging trends, readers will gain insights into the skills and technologies that will be essential for future cybercrime investigators. This chapter aims to equip readers with the foresight needed to anticipate challenges and remain proactive in safeguarding against the next generation of cyber threats, ultimately reinforcing the importance of continuous learning and adaptation in the ever-evolving world of cybercrime.

## 12.1 The Future of Ransomware: Anticipating New Tactics

Ransomware has emerged as one of the most formidable threats in the cyber landscape, inflicting devastating impacts on individuals, businesses, and governmental organizations alike. As cybercriminals refine their strategies and exploit new vulnerabilities, the future of ransomware is expected to evolve significantly. This section explores potential future tactics of ransomware attackers, the factors driving these changes, and the implications for organizations striving to defend against this insidious threat.

### 1. The Evolving Landscape of Ransomware

The past few years have witnessed a marked evolution in ransomware tactics. Initially, ransomware primarily relied on encrypting data to hold it hostage until a ransom was paid. However, as defenses have improved, cybercriminals have adopted more sophisticated and multi-faceted approaches. Some key trends in the evolving ransomware landscape include:

**Double and Triple Extortion**: Attackers have increasingly adopted double extortion tactics, where they not only encrypt data but also exfiltrate sensitive information, threatening to publish it unless the ransom is paid. This strategy has forced organizations to consider not only the financial implications of data loss but also reputational damage.

In some cases, triple extortion is being employed, wherein attackers also target third parties, such as customers or partners, to further pressure the victim into compliance.

**Targeting Critical Infrastructure**: Ransomware attacks have increasingly targeted critical infrastructure sectors, such as healthcare, energy, and transportation. These sectors often have higher stakes, as downtime can lead to significant consequences for public safety and national security. As attackers recognize the value of disrupting essential services, they are likely to focus more on these high-impact targets.

**Ransomware-as-a-Service (RaaS):** The emergence of Ransomware-as-a-Service platforms has made it easier for less technically skilled criminals to execute attacks. RaaS allows affiliates to launch ransomware campaigns using sophisticated tools and infrastructures developed by more experienced cybercriminals. This commoditization of ransomware has led to an increase in the frequency and scale of attacks.

## 2. Anticipating New Tactics

As ransomware continues to evolve, organizations must anticipate new tactics that attackers may employ. Several potential future tactics include:

**Enhanced Sophistication in Encryption Methods**: As cybersecurity defenses improve, attackers may develop more advanced encryption algorithms that are harder to break without the decryption keys. This could involve using strong encryption coupled with steganography to conceal ransomware payloads within seemingly benign files, making detection more challenging.

**Leveraging Artificial Intelligence and Machine Learning**: Cybercriminals may increasingly leverage artificial intelligence (AI) and machine learning (ML) to optimize their ransomware campaigns. These technologies can help attackers identify vulnerabilities, automate reconnaissance, and tailor their attacks to specific targets. AI-powered ransomware could dynamically adapt its tactics based on the defenses it encounters, making it more resilient against detection and mitigation efforts.

**Exploitation of Supply Chain Vulnerabilities**: Ransomware attackers may shift their focus to exploiting vulnerabilities in supply chains, as seen in attacks like the Colonial Pipeline incident. By targeting third-party vendors and service providers, attackers can infiltrate organizations with stronger defenses, effectively bypassing traditional perimeter security measures.

**Integration with Other Cybercrime Tactics**: Future ransomware attacks may increasingly integrate with other cybercrime tactics, such as Distributed Denial of Service (DDoS) attacks or credential stuffing. For example, an attacker may initiate a DDoS attack against an organization to distract security teams while deploying ransomware in the background. This multi-pronged approach could complicate incident response efforts and increase the likelihood of successful attacks.

**Social Engineering and Phishing Innovations**: As organizations enhance their technical defenses, attackers may rely more heavily on social engineering tactics to trick individuals into enabling ransomware. Future phishing attacks may become increasingly sophisticated, leveraging AI-generated content to create highly personalized and convincing messages that are more likely to deceive victims.

### 3. Implications for Organizations

The anticipated evolution of ransomware tactics has significant implications for organizations, requiring a proactive and multi-faceted approach to cybersecurity:

**Investing in Cybersecurity Awareness Training**: Organizations must prioritize employee education to enhance their resilience against social engineering attacks. Regular training sessions that simulate phishing scenarios can help employees recognize and respond to potential threats.

**Strengthening Incident Response Plans**: Developing and regularly updating incident response plans is crucial for effectively addressing ransomware attacks. Organizations should conduct tabletop exercises to test their response capabilities and ensure that all stakeholders understand their roles during an incident.

**Implementing Advanced Threat Detection**: Organizations should invest in advanced threat detection and response solutions that leverage AI and machine learning to identify anomalies and potential ransomware activity in real time. Integrating these solutions with existing security tools can enhance overall visibility and response capabilities.

**Enhancing Backup and Recovery Strategies**: Regularly backing up critical data and implementing robust recovery processes are essential for mitigating the impact of ransomware. Organizations should store backups offline and test their restoration procedures to ensure they can recover quickly without paying ransoms.

**Collaboration and Information Sharing**: Engaging with industry partners, law enforcement, and information-sharing organizations can provide valuable insights into emerging threats and best practices for defending against ransomware. Collaborating with others in the same industry can help organizations stay informed about the latest attack vectors and tactics.

The future of ransomware presents a complex and evolving landscape, characterized by increasingly sophisticated tactics and a growing reliance on technological advancements. To effectively combat these threats, organizations must anticipate potential changes and adapt their cybersecurity strategies accordingly. By investing in employee training, enhancing incident response capabilities, and leveraging advanced technologies, organizations can strengthen their defenses against the looming threat of ransomware. As the cybercrime landscape continues to evolve, proactive measures and collaboration will be key in the ongoing battle against ransomware and its devastating impact on individuals and society.

## 12.2 Evolving Cybersecurity Measures: Staying Ahead

As cyber threats grow more sophisticated and pervasive, organizations must adopt evolving cybersecurity measures to stay ahead of attackers. The dynamic nature of cybercrime demands a proactive approach that anticipates potential vulnerabilities and leverages advanced technologies to fortify defenses. This section explores key trends in cybersecurity, innovative strategies to combat emerging threats, and the importance of continuous adaptation to safeguard critical assets.

**1. The Changing Cyber Threat Landscape**

The landscape of cyber threats is continually shifting, driven by several factors:

**Increased Attack Surface**: The rise of remote work, cloud computing, and the Internet of Things (IoT) has significantly expanded the attack surface. With more devices and users connected to corporate networks, attackers have a broader range of entry points to exploit.

**Sophisticated Attack Techniques**: Cybercriminals are increasingly using advanced techniques such as artificial intelligence (AI) and machine learning (ML) to enhance their attacks. This includes developing more effective phishing campaigns, automating the exploitation of vulnerabilities, and creating malware that can adapt to evade detection.

**Motivations Beyond Financial Gain**: While financial motivations remain a primary driver of cybercrime, other factors are emerging. State-sponsored actors, hacktivists, and cyber terrorists have entered the arena, leading to attacks motivated by political, ideological, or social agendas. This diversification complicates the threat landscape and increases the urgency for organizations to bolster their defenses.

## 2. Key Trends in Cybersecurity Measures

To address these evolving threats, organizations are implementing several key trends in cybersecurity measures:

**Zero Trust Architecture**: The Zero Trust model is gaining traction as organizations recognize the limitations of traditional perimeter-based security. Zero Trust operates on the principle of "never trust, always verify," meaning that every user and device must be authenticated and authorized before accessing resources. This model enhances security by reducing the risk of insider threats and lateral movement within networks.

**Extended Detection and Response (XDR):** XDR is an integrated security approach that consolidates multiple security tools and data sources to provide a more comprehensive view of threats across an organization's environment. By correlating data from endpoints, networks, and servers, XDR enables faster detection, investigation, and response to threats.

**Artificial Intelligence and Machine Learning**: AI and ML are playing increasingly significant roles in cybersecurity. These technologies can analyze vast amounts of data to identify patterns, detect anomalies, and respond to threats in real time. AI-driven solutions can enhance threat intelligence, automate responses, and improve overall security posture.

**Automated Threat Hunting**: As the volume of threats increases, organizations are turning to automated threat hunting to proactively identify potential risks. These automated systems can analyze network traffic and user behavior to detect suspicious activities before they escalate into significant incidents.

**Cloud Security Posture Management (CSPM):** With the widespread adoption of cloud services, organizations are prioritizing cloud security. CSPM solutions continuously assess cloud configurations and identify vulnerabilities, ensuring that security policies are consistently applied and maintained across cloud environments.

## 3. Innovative Strategies for Cybersecurity

In addition to these trends, organizations are adopting innovative strategies to enhance their cybersecurity measures:

**Threat Intelligence Sharing**: Collaboration and information sharing among organizations, government agencies, and industry groups are becoming critical components of cybersecurity strategies. By sharing threat intelligence, organizations can gain insights into emerging threats and vulnerabilities, enabling them to bolster their defenses and respond more effectively.

**Red and Blue Team Exercises**: Engaging in red team (offensive) and blue team (defensive) exercises allows organizations to simulate real-world attack scenarios. Red teams test the organization's defenses, while blue teams respond and strengthen security measures. This practice fosters a culture of continuous improvement and enhances incident response capabilities.

**Security Awareness Training**: Employees are often the weakest link in cybersecurity. Organizations are increasingly investing in comprehensive security awareness training programs to educate staff about common threats, such as phishing and social engineering, and promote a security-first mindset.

**Regular Vulnerability Assessments and Penetration Testing**: Conducting regular vulnerability assessments and penetration tests helps organizations identify weaknesses in their systems before attackers can exploit them. By proactively addressing vulnerabilities, organizations can strengthen their overall security posture.

## 4. Continuous Adaptation to Cybersecurity Challenges

To stay ahead of evolving cyber threats, organizations must adopt a mindset of continuous adaptation. This involves:

**Ongoing Risk Assessments**: Regularly assessing risks and vulnerabilities allows organizations to identify emerging threats and adjust their security measures accordingly. A proactive approach to risk management helps prioritize resources and ensures that defenses remain effective.

**Agile Security Practices**: Embracing agile methodologies can enhance the responsiveness of cybersecurity teams. Agile security practices enable organizations to quickly adapt to changing threats, implement new security measures, and respond to incidents in real time.

**Investing in Research and Development**: Organizations should allocate resources to research and development efforts aimed at identifying new security technologies and strategies. Staying informed about emerging trends and threats can help organizations remain ahead of attackers.

**Collaboration with Cybersecurity Experts**: Partnering with cybersecurity experts, including consultants, managed security service providers (MSSPs), and threat intelligence organizations, can provide valuable insights and bolster an organization's security measures.

As cyber threats continue to evolve, organizations must proactively adopt evolving cybersecurity measures to safeguard their critical assets. By leveraging key trends such as Zero Trust architecture, AI and ML technologies, and automated threat hunting, organizations can enhance their defenses against sophisticated attacks. Additionally, implementing innovative strategies, engaging in continuous adaptation, and fostering a culture of security awareness will empower organizations to stay ahead of cybercriminals. In an increasingly interconnected world, the commitment to robust cybersecurity practices is not just a matter of compliance; it is essential for maintaining trust, protecting sensitive data, and ensuring business continuity. As the cyber landscape evolves, organizations that prioritize proactive measures and continuous improvement will be better positioned to face the challenges ahead.

## 12.3 The Role of Artificial Intelligence in Future Investigations

Artificial Intelligence (AI) is transforming various sectors, including law enforcement, cybersecurity, and digital forensics. As cybercrime becomes more sophisticated, the integration of AI technologies in investigations is proving crucial for enhancing efficiency, accuracy, and effectiveness. This section explores the evolving role of AI in future investigations, highlighting its potential applications, benefits, challenges, and implications for investigators and law enforcement agencies.

### 1. AI Applications in Investigative Processes

AI can be leveraged in various stages of investigations, offering significant enhancements to traditional methods. Some key applications include:

**Data Analysis and Pattern Recognition**: One of the primary strengths of AI lies in its ability to analyze vast amounts of data quickly and identify patterns that human investigators might overlook. Machine learning algorithms can sift through extensive datasets—such as transaction records, social media interactions, and network traffic—unearthing connections and anomalies indicative of criminal activity.

**Predictive Analytics**: AI systems can analyze historical data to predict future criminal activities, allowing law enforcement agencies to allocate resources more effectively. By identifying hotspots of criminal activity and understanding emerging trends, AI can help agencies preemptively respond to potential threats.

**Natural Language Processing (NLP)**: NLP enables AI systems to analyze unstructured data sources, such as emails, chat logs, and social media posts. By extracting relevant information and sentiments from these texts, investigators can gain insights into criminal intent, networks, and communication patterns.

**Automated Threat Detection**: AI-driven security systems can continuously monitor networks for suspicious activities, flagging anomalies in real-time. These systems use machine learning algorithms to adapt and improve their detection capabilities based on evolving threats, enabling faster responses to cyber incidents.

**Facial Recognition and Image Analysis**: AI technologies, including facial recognition systems, are increasingly employed in investigations to identify suspects in security footage or social media images. Image recognition algorithms can also analyze photographs for evidence, such as identifying locations or objects that may link to a crime.

## 2. Benefits of AI in Investigations

The integration of AI into investigative processes offers numerous benefits:

**Increased Efficiency**: AI can process and analyze data at speeds far beyond human capabilities. This efficiency allows investigators to focus their time on strategic analysis rather than manual data review, speeding up the investigation timeline.

**Enhanced Accuracy**: AI algorithms can minimize human error by providing consistent and objective analysis of data. By reducing bias and improving accuracy, AI can lead to more reliable conclusions and evidence in investigations.

**Scalability**: As the volume of digital data continues to grow, AI systems can scale to handle large datasets without compromising performance. This scalability is crucial for investigations that require analyzing vast amounts of information from various sources.

**Resource Optimization**: By automating routine tasks, AI enables investigators to prioritize high-value work. This optimization of resources can lead to better outcomes, as investigators can dedicate more time to complex problem-solving and strategic planning.

## 3. Challenges in Implementing AI Technologies

Despite the numerous benefits, the adoption of AI in investigations is not without challenges:

**Data Privacy Concerns**: The use of AI technologies raises significant data privacy issues. Investigators must navigate complex legal frameworks and ethical considerations when handling sensitive personal data. Ensuring compliance with data protection regulations is crucial to maintain public trust.

**Bias in Algorithms**: AI systems are only as good as the data they are trained on. If historical data contains biases, these can be perpetuated in AI models, leading to skewed results and potentially discriminatory practices in investigations. Addressing bias in AI algorithms is essential for fair and just outcomes.

**Complexity and Integration**: Integrating AI technologies into existing investigative processes can be complex. Organizations must invest in training personnel to understand and effectively utilize these tools, as well as ensure seamless integration with current systems and workflows.

**Reliance on Technology**: Over-reliance on AI may lead to complacency among investigators. While AI can enhance investigations, it is crucial to maintain a balance between technological tools and human judgment, ensuring that critical thinking and expertise remain at the forefront of investigative efforts.

## 4. Future Implications of AI in Investigations

As AI continues to evolve, its role in investigations will likely expand and deepen. Some potential future implications include:

**Greater Collaboration Between Humans and AI**: The future of investigations will likely see a hybrid model where human investigators work alongside AI systems. This collaboration can leverage the strengths of both, with AI providing insights and support while human judgment guides decision-making.

**Continuous Learning and Adaptation**: AI systems will increasingly utilize machine learning to refine their algorithms based on feedback from investigations. This continuous learning process will enhance the accuracy and reliability of AI tools, making them invaluable assets in future investigations.

**Integration with Emerging Technologies**: AI will likely be integrated with other emerging technologies, such as blockchain and the Internet of Things (IoT), to create a more comprehensive investigative framework. For example, blockchain technology could provide secure, immutable records of evidence, while AI analyzes these records for insights.

**Focus on Proactive Investigations**: With the ability to predict and detect potential criminal activities, AI may shift the focus of investigations from reactive measures to proactive strategies. This shift could lead to earlier intervention in criminal activities, ultimately preventing crimes before they occur.

Artificial Intelligence is poised to play a transformative role in future investigations, enhancing efficiency, accuracy, and effectiveness across various stages of the investigative process. By leveraging AI technologies for data analysis, predictive analytics, and automated threat detection, investigators can stay ahead of evolving cyber threats. However, challenges related to data privacy, algorithmic bias, and reliance on technology must be addressed to ensure ethical and fair outcomes. As the landscape of crime continues to evolve, the collaboration between human investigators and AI systems will be crucial in adapting to new challenges and safeguarding society against the ever-growing threat of cybercrime. Embracing AI as a valuable partner in investigations will empower law enforcement and cyber investigators to respond effectively to the complex and dynamic nature of modern crime.

In **Digital Detectives: Strategies for Uncovering Cybercrime Evidence**, Dmitry Popovyzu offers a comprehensive and practical guide to navigating the complexities of cybercrime investigations. As our reliance on technology grows, so too does the prevalence of cyber threats, making it imperative for individuals and organizations to be equipped with the knowledge and skills necessary to combat these challenges.

Throughout the book, readers will explore the evolution of cybercrime, from its early days to the sophisticated tactics employed by today's cybercriminals. By delving into essential frameworks, digital forensics principles, and evidence collection techniques, this book empowers readers to uncover the truth behind cyber incidents effectively.

Dmitry combines theoretical insights with real-world case studies, illustrating successful investigation strategies and highlighting the lessons learned from past experiences. Each chapter emphasizes the importance of a multidisciplinary approach, covering legal considerations, social media dynamics, and the impact of emerging technologies on cybersecurity.

Whether you are a law enforcement officer, cybersecurity professional, or simply an informed citizen, Digital Detectives provides the tools and strategies needed to become an effective digital detective. As you turn the final pages of this book, you will be better prepared to confront the ever-evolving landscape of cybercrime, armed with practical knowledge and insights that will enhance your ability to protect and serve in the digital realm.

In the face of increasing cyber threats, the journey of a digital detective is just beginning. Equip yourself with the strategies from this book, and be ready to uncover the hidden truths of our interconnected world.

www.ingramcontent.com/pod-product-compliance
Lightning Source LLC
Chambersburg PA
CBHW062106220526
45471CB00010B/3622